PRESENTATION SKILLS:
One Hour Workshop

Carol A. Silvis, M.Ed.

Cengage Learning PTR

CENGAGE
Learning·

Professional • Technical • Reference

Australia, Brazil, Japan, Korea, Mexico, Singapore, Spain, United Kingdom, United States

CENGAGE
Learning·

Professional • Technical • Reference

Presentation Skills:
One Hour Workshop
Carol A. Silvis, M.Ed.

Publisher and General Manager,
Cengage Learning PTR:
Stacy L. Hiquet

Associate Director of Marketing:
Sarah Panella

Manager of Editorial Services:
Heather Talbot

Senior Product Manager:
Mitzi Koontz

Project and Copy Editor:
Karen A. Gill

Interior Layout:
Shawn Morningstar

Cover Designer:
Luke Fletcher

Proofreader:
Sue Boshers

For product information and technology assistance, contact us at **Cengage Learning Customer & Sales Support, 1-800-354-9706.**

For permission to use material from this text or product, submit all requests online at **cengage.com/permissions.**

Further permissions questions can be emailed to **permissionrequest@cengage.com.**

Library of Congress Control Number: 2014954907

ISBN-13: 978-1-305-50741-8

ISBN-10: 1-305-50741-X

Cengage Learning PTR
20 Channel Center Street
Boston, MA 02210
USA

Cengage Learning is a leading provider of customized learning solutions with office locations around the globe, including Singapore, the United Kingdom, Australia, Mexico, Brazil, and Japan. Locate your local office at: **international.cengage.com/region.**

Cengage Learning products are represented in Canada by Nelson Education, Ltd.

For your lifelong learning solutions, visit **cengageptr.com.**

Visit our corporate website at **cengage.com.**

Printed in the United States of America
Print Number: 01   Print Year: 2015

This book is dedicated to my family, Ryan, Niki, and Mikaila,
who encourage and inspire me every day.

Acknowledgments

A special thanks to Mitzi Koontz, senior product manager, for her vision and support with this project, and to Karen Gill, project and copy editor, for her expertise and assistance. It is a pleasure to work with such dedicated professionals. Thanks also to the many others who had a hand in producing this book.

About the Author

Carol A. Silvis, M.Ed. is the author of *101 Ways to Connect with Customers, Chiefs, and Coworkers*; *Job Hunting After 50*; *101 Ways to Make Yourself Indispensable at Work*; and *100% Externship Success and General Office Procedures*, all available through Cengage Learning. Other publications include "Time Management and Organization for Writers" (2012 *Writers Market*), a dozen creative nonfiction stories and inspirational pieces published in national magazines, and more than 40 articles published in various newsletters.

Carol has been interviewed for Yahoo.com, AARP online, CBSMoneywatch.com, ABCNews.com, and *Writer's Digest*; she has also appeared on Cornerstone TV, HMC-TV, and WIUP-TV.

She has a master's in education and has trained adults in how to get a job, keep and enjoy it, and get ahead. She gives workshops and seminars for schools, businesses, professional organizations, and libraries on a wide range of business topics.

Carol is the president of Pennwriters, Inc., coordinating her third conference. In 2008, she received the Meritorious Service Award.

Visit her website at www.carolsilvis.com and her blog at www.carolsilvis.blogspot.com.

Table of Contents

Part I
Effective Presentations   1

Chapter 1 Planning and Organizing   3

Chapter 2 Writing the Text   19

Chapter 3 Developing Visual Aids   31

Part II
Facilities   41

Chapter 4 Learning About the Venue, Room Layout,
and Amenities   43

Chapter 5 Dressing for the Part 51

Part III
Delivering the Content 57

Chapter 6 Focusing on Your Audience 59

Chapter 7 Perfecting Your Delivery Method and Pacing   67

Chapter 8 Practicing Your Presentation   79

Chapter 9 Delivering the Speech and the Wrap-Up   89

Chapter 10　Improving Through Evaluations　　97

Chapter 11　Building a Platform　　105

Introduction

Effective presenters are focused, well-prepared experts on their topics. They deliver noteworthy messages in a professional manner. They and their messages are remembered by their audiences.

Unfortunately, many presenters deliver boring, unpassionate, indifferent presentations that trap their audiences with a dreary speech and dreadful visuals. Everyone loses to some degree during a poor presentation.

Being an excellent presenter can give your career a boost and bring you opportunities. Whether your presentation is for a large or small, formal or informal event, choose an appropriate topic, research it thoroughly, prepare audiovisuals and handouts to accompany your talk, and practice your presentation all the while being mindful of your allotted time. These aspects are discussed throughout this book.

Practicing your presentation and using correct techniques can enhance your skills. Follow the suggestions and guidelines outlined in the following chapters to improve your presentation performance.

How This Book Is Organized

This book offers tips and guidelines for giving better presentations as well as exercises and checklists to help the reader put the ideas they read about into practice. Chapter 1, "Planning and Organizing," discusses the importance of preparation before a presentation. Chapter 2, "Writing the Text," gives pointers for preparing better content. Chapter 3, "Developing Visual Aids," provides guidelines for making visuals that will complement your talk and keep the audience engaged. Chapter 4, "Learning About the Venue, Room Layout, and Amenities," advises becoming familiar with the venue before the presentation. Chapter 5, "Dressing for the Part," suggests ways to present a successful appearance that leaves a positive impression on the audience. Chapter 6, "Focusing on Your Audience," recommends ways to gain and hold your audience's attention. Chapter 7, "Perfecting Your Delivery Method and Pacing," provides tips for orally presenting the information to an audience. Chapter 8, "Practicing Your Presentation," stresses the importance of practicing before stepping in front of your audience. Chapter 9, "Delivering the Speech and the Wrap-Up," recommends ways to deliver a winning presentation. Chapter 10, "Improving Through Evaluations," points out the value of having the audience evaluate your presentation. Chapter 11, "Building a Platform," suggests ways to make people aware of your speaking skills and your availability to give future presentations.

The suggestions in this book guide the reader in learning how to be a better speaker and presenter.

Who This Book Is For

This book will benefit people who must speak to individuals and groups. The information presented is intended for speakers who are just starting out and for those who want to improve their presentation skills.

PART I

Effective Presentations

CHAPTER 1

Planning and Organizing

Fear of public speaking is high on the list of fears for most people. However, it is critical to personal and professional success to be able to express yourself clearly when speaking to others. We rely on speaking to others not only in our personal lives, but in our work lives as we communicate with coworkers, supervisors, customers, and other associates.

Learning beneficial tips and techniques can help ease fears and nervousness. The more prepared you are, the easier it will be to deliver a great presentation and persuade your audience to act or react in a particular way. As with any skill, applying proper techniques and practicing will help you improve and become a better presenter.

You may be an expert in your field and have a wealth of information to pass on to others, but if you do not convey it effectively in a manner that will hold your audience's attention, your message and purpose will be lost.

You may be called upon to give informal and formal presentations and talks during your career in a variety of situations, including these:

- ✦ Updating your supervisor and coworkers on the progress of tasks
- ✦ Presenting sales or marketing figures
- ✦ Facilitating company training programs
- ✦ Giving workshops and seminars
- ✦ Lecturing or teaching
- ✦ Giving instructions
- ✦ Presenting information to small or large groups
- ✦ Advising customers and clients
- ✦ Selling to customers and clients
- ✦ Presiding over meetings
- ✦ Mentoring
- ✦ Speaking to students and interns
- ✦ Speaking to professional organizations in your field
- ✦ Directing or overseeing community events
- ✦ Giving or conducting interviews
- ✦ Negotiating
- ✦ Conducting or participating in performance reviews
- ✦ Introducing speakers and presenters
- ✦ Giving a dinner speech

ACCEPTING THE CHALLENGE

You may be called upon to present information, disseminate knowledge, or teach skills in situations ranging from small and large meetings to workshops and conferences. Conveying information in a way that engages your audience can be the difference between communicating with them and failing to connect. The more effectively you can communicate, the more people will want to hear what you have to say. Improve your effectiveness by planning and organizing your presentation from beginning to end.

Do not mistake an informal presentation for an effortless presentation. Oftentimes, presenting in an informal setting comes with pitfalls. For instance, you may feel more relaxed and inadvertently give your audience the impression that your topic is not important. If your audience is made up of your peers, you may feel extra pressure to perform well.

Formal presentations afford an opportunity to display your expertise to large numbers of people. Unfortunately, it can be a painful experience if your presentation is a flop. Do your part to ensure success through thorough planning and preparation.

Besides devoting attention to what you will say and how you will present the information, learn as much as you can about the event. Why is the event being held? What is expected of you and the other presenters? Find out about the purpose of the event, your topic, and other topics being presented. Knowing the other speakers' topics will help you avoid overlapping your information with theirs. What about the venue? If the setting is unfamiliar, ask about the setup of the room, audiovisual support, and any special needs you may have.

Exercise: Assess Your Feelings

You are asked to give a presentation. Do you know to whom you are speaking and why? What are your feelings toward the size and type of audience? Consider the following scenarios:

+ You are asked to give a formal presentation to a group of 50 professionals in your field.

+ You are asked to present a new product to several clients.

+ You are asked to give a sales presentation to your department. You will discuss sales figures, new products, and outdated products.

+ You are the keynote for an educational conference with hundreds of attendees.

For each one of these presentations, decide how you would answer the following questions:

Are you more comfortable speaking to a small or a large group? _____

Are you more comfortable speaking to coworkers and supervisors or strangers? _____

Are you comfortable speaking on a topic for which you are an expert? _____

How does it make you feel to know you will be in the spotlight for the length of the presentation?

_____

_____

_____

Are you cool and collected or nervous and stressed when you present? _____

Do you imagine you will know what you want to say, or will you forget most of it? _____

_____

How do you react when asked to speak in front of your peers? _____

_____

_____

_____

How do you react when asked to speak to a large audience of strangers? _____

_____

_____

_____

_____

GETTING PREPARED

Planning is a critical step in creating a successful presentation, whether for an audience of a few or hundreds. Effective planning helps you gather content, lay it out in a logical sequence, and present it in a results-oriented manner. You will be clear on the concepts you want to present and those your audience needs to hear. A successful presentation will allow you to contribute to others in an influential, positive manner.

Preparation is necessary if you want to deliver a clear message that impacts your audience in a meaningful way, whether the audience is one person or hundreds. If your message is not clear or your facts are distorted, you will not be convincing, and your audience may miss key information. Any time your audience questions what you are saying, you lose the audience for that period of time.

Solid preparation and practice can turn an average or below-average presentation into an excellent one. Lay the correct groundwork by doing everything you can to create an exceptional presentation. Do not settle for good enough—aim for the best. From selecting a topic to researching to organizing to readying yourself, be prepared. It is far better to be over-prepared than to be under-prepared no matter what the speaking occasion. This chapter and the following ones will present guidelines for preparing and delivering first-class presentations.

What do you hope to accomplish with your presentation? Knowing what you want to get across to your audience will help you formulate clear ideas and specifics. From there you can build a convincing case to persuade your audience to act or react the way you intend.

Know your material well, but do not memorize it. Regurgitating a memorized speech could cause you to speak in a monotone, to rush through the material, or to seem unapproachable. Keep in mind that your audience is there to learn from you. Do not talk over their heads or use jargon they may not understand. It is your job as a speaker to present information in a way that your listeners can understand your message. Chapter 2, "Writing the Text," discusses ways to get your written message across to your audience. With sufficient preparation, you will be able to gear your speech to the audience.

PLANNING YOUR PRESENTATION

Regardless of the type of presentation, plan to the fullest extent. First of all, make sure you understand what is required of you and what you are expected to deliver to the audience. Miscommunication can lead to embarrassment and a failed presentation. Ask:

◆ Am I clear about what specifically the organizers want me to communicate?

◆ What are the organizers trying to achieve through this presentation?

◆ Why have the organizers chosen me to present this information?

♦ Do I have the ability to meet the organizer's objectives for the presentation?

♦ Am I willing to meet the organizer's objectives for the presentation?

Effective presentations require significant planning. Take the time to prepare from the day you know you will be presenting. Avoid procrastinating. You will want as much time as possible to research and practice. When you have a long lead time before your presentation, brainstorm ideas and begin your research. The more you prepare, the better your presentation will likely be.

Treat all presentations, formal and informal, as important. Do not be fooled into thinking an informal presentation for your coworkers or for a single client is not important enough to plan. Many of the one-on-one talks are critical to career success.

Spend time thinking about what you want to say and what the audience needs to hear. You want to be able to convey your message in the clearest, most convincing way possible. If you cannot convince your audience, you cannot accomplish your goal. If you cannot get your ideas across to others, you will not be able to engage your audience and share information. To keep your audience engaged, you will want to convey information relevant to them quickly and succinctly. The best way to do this is through thorough preparation. Question everything that will go into making your presentation a success.

Prepare by asking yourself the following key questions:

♦ What is the event, and where is it being held?

♦ What is the layout of the venue?

♦ Is it a formal or an informal event?

♦ What is the purpose of the presentation?

♦ Why am I the best person to present the information?

♦ What is my topic?

♦ What key points about the topic must I include?

♦ How much research do I need to do?

♦ Do I need to consult other sources (colleagues, experts in the subject, and so on)?

♦ Who is my intended audience, and how large is the group?

♦ What does my audience expect from the presentation?

♦ Does my audience know anything about my topic?

♦ How will I create interest?

♦ How will I hold my audience's attention throughout the presentation?

♦ What is the best way to organize my message?

♦ What visual aids will I utilize?

♦ What audio visual or other equipment do I need?

♦ What handouts will I prepare?

♦ What are three to five main points I want my audience to remember at the end of my presentation?

♦ What action do I want the audience to take, or how do I want them to react?

♦ How will I dress for the presentation?

After you know the type of event and venue, you can decide on an effective method of delivery. For instance, a small meeting may not require substantial visual aids, whereas a large audience may require a high-tech delivery system.

You will need to know what is expected from you as a presenter. Are you selling something? Are you teaching a skill? Do you have vital information to deliver? Will you suggest solutions to problems? You will take a different approach in these and other diverse situations.

Know your time limit, and pace yourself accordingly. Will your message be brief? Are you giving a two-hour workshop? Do you have a time slot between other speakers? Do you need to allow time for interaction with your audience or for a question-and-answer session? In addition, you should plan for unforeseen distractions and interruptions. A number of things can throw off your timing.

Complete the following checklist.

Checklist for Effective Planning	Yes	No
I have a well-defined topic.		
I know the purpose of my presentation.		
I know the type of event and venue.		
I know what material I need to present.		
I know what the organizers want to accomplish with this presentation.		
I know something of the audience's backgrounds and knowledge of my topic.		
I have an idea of what the audience expects from this presentation.		
I know the size of the group.		
I have an idea of what handouts I will prepare.		
I have an idea of what visual aids I will prepare.		
I know what research I need to complete.		
I know what sources I will use for my research.		
I know the key points I want to discuss.		
I know how to organize my message.		
I have thought about ways to create audience interest.		
I know what I want my audience to take away from this presentation.		
I know how I want my audience to act or react following my presentation.		
I have chosen an outfit for the event.		

You should have answered yes to each item in the checklist. Work toward correcting any negative answers.

Exercise: Plan a Presentation

The next time you are called upon to give a presentation, complete the following exercise.

Presentation topic _____

Purpose of my presentation

_____

_____

_____

Type of event and venue

_____

_____

What I hope to accomplish

_____

_____

_____

Size and background of audience

_____

_____

_____

What I think the audience expects from the presentation

_____

_____

_____

Key points I will discuss

_____

_____

_____

Research sources I will use

_____

_____

_____

How I will create interest

_____

_____

_____

How I will organize my presentation

_____

_____

_____

Handouts and visuals I will use

_____

_____

_____

What I would like the audience to gain

_____

_____

_____

Brainstorm Ideas

Brainstorming allows you to produce lots of information quickly without judging the ideas as good or bad. List your topic at the top of a piece of paper (or on a whiteboard if you are brainstorming with others). Write down as many ideas as you can think of concerning your topic as well as ideas for supporting information. Do not dismiss concepts you believe are worthless at first thought. They may turn out to be the best ones in the long run. The idea is to write everything down and later eliminate whatever you feel will be useless for your presentation. It is easier to cut ideas than it is to come up with them in the first place.

If other people are involved in the presentation, ask for their input. Add facts from anyone else who might have something relevant to contribute. Add information from other sources. The more ideas you have, the greater the chance of finding the important, dynamic ones that will make your presentation resonate with your audience.

If other speakers are participating in the event, check that your topic and ideas are not redundant. Although speakers for a particular event may be presenting along the same line, you will not want to repeat another participant's presentation.

Choose the Best Ideas

After compiling your idea list, trim it to three to five key points. Write down your topic sentence. Branch out from there by choosing relevant key points. Think about the information that will be most useful to your audience.

Although you may feel that all of your ideas are important, you have a limited amount of time. You must focus; your audience will tune you out if they are overloaded with information. Concentrating on a few relevant concepts will keep your audience from becoming overwhelmed and distracted. Limiting information will also help you avoid jumping from point to point in a confusing manner.

Exercise: Brainstorm Ideas for Your Presentation

Create three headings: Introduction, Main Body, Conclusion. Under each of the headings, list what you would like to cover during your presentation. Concentrate your key points in the main body.

Exercise: Choose Ideas for Your Presentation

The next time you are called upon to give a presentation, complete the following exercise.

Presentation topic _____

Brainstorming ideas

_____

_____

_____

_____

_____

_____

From your list of brainstorm ideas, write down three to five key points to cover and how you will support them.

1. _____

_____

_____

_____

2. _____
   _____
   _____
   _____
   _____
   _____

3. _____
   _____
   _____
   _____
   _____
   _____

4. _____
   _____
   _____
   _____
   _____
   _____

5. _____
   _____
   _____
   _____
   _____
   _____

Gather the Content

All effective presentations are based on meaningful content appropriate for the audience. To avoid omitting important information, create a detailed list of everything you definitely must cover, and build your talk around this list. Review what you know about your topic, and write it down in a logical order. Take care to avoid recycling information from former presentations or sources that may be outdated.

In addition to counting on your own expertise, some places to gather content include company materials, journals and magazines, books, colleagues, and other experts in the field.

Do Your Research

Research the latest information on your topic, and add it to what you know. Uncovering innovative, original information will give you a fresh perspective and ensure that your audience is given the latest facts. Extensive research gives you a solid foundation on which to build your presentation and from which to choose supporting data for your essential key points. All researched information must be current and credible; take the time to get your facts right, and double-check your sources.

Make your content relevant to your audience. How do you plan to address their needs? No one wants to waste time hearing you talk about something that has nothing to do with them. Is the information you plan to present the information your reader needs and wants to hear? Each audience and speaking opportunity is different; plan accordingly.

Although you should limit the information you deliver to a few key points, gathering as many facts as possible about your topic will give you an abundance of research from which to develop your presentation. This extra information will be useful when you are called upon to discuss a particular point or to answer questions. Know your material well so you will not be caught off guard by someone questioning your facts or during the discussion or the question-and-answer session.

Focus on your topic, taking a narrow approach to the treatment of the subject. You will want to select vital information and eliminate the extraneous from the talk itself. Enhance your subject with supporting evidence to build believability, but keep everything focused on the key points.

Look for unusual and interesting facts and figures that will excite your audience, not bore them. Oftentimes a little-known fact is enough for people to sit up and take notice. Limit the content of your talk to uncomplicated material and the essential facts and figures. Your audience may become disinterested if your presentation is too heavy on figures, charts, complicated facts, and long passages of dull material.

Consult company materials when developing a company-based presentation. Read the latest journals in your field, and scour newspapers and magazines for useful articles. Textbooks and business books might provide valuable facts, illustrations, statistics, and additional research sources.

Colleagues in the field and coworkers can be good resources for information to round out your talk. Make sure they are authorities on the subject and their information is up to date and credible. Resist the urge to use someone else's presentation, as you may not be able to deliver the information successfully when it is not yours.

The Internet is another good source of information. Type your topic into a search engine, but be selective. Much of the information on the Internet is written by individuals who have no expertise in the area or no credentials in the field. Be sure to consult highly regarded, well-known sites that are most likely to have accurate information. If you find information you can use, you can view it or store it on your computer or print it out. Be aware that this information could run several printed pages. Do not commit plagiarism by taking someone else's work as your own or infringe on a copyright.

Always cite sources. Keeping track of where you find information will be helpful when you need to make the citations in your presentation. Use a spreadsheet or similar format to record source information.

Exercise: Research Sources

The next time you are called on to give a presentation, create a list of viable sources to use for researching your topic.

Decide on Content

Sort through your notes, and decide what the single most important point is for you to cover. What is the next important point? Jot down items you want to discuss and those you want to reinforce. Include challenges, solutions, action the audience should take, consequences for failing to act or react, and benefits of taking appropriate action. Content for each of your key points should be limited to critical information. You want enough information to support your point, but this is not the time to share everything there is about the subject. Skip unimportant details and less relevant information. Include information that supports your topic and delivers what the audience came to learn.

Overloading the presentation by attempting to cram in every detail about the topic could cause you to overrun your time limit and cause the audience to quit listening. Advance planning will help you determine suitable content that conveys the essence of your message.

Complete the following checklist.

Content Checklist	Yes	No
I have narrowed the focus of my talk and decided the most important point I want to cover.		
I have limited key points to three to five.		
I have focused my talk on what I believe is important to my audience.		
I have thoroughly researched my topic.		
I have found sufficient information to support my key points.		
I have found unusual, interesting facts.		
I have eliminated irrelevant information from my talk.		
I have checked all my sources.		
I have given proper credit to my sources.		
I have not plagiarized or infringed on any copyrights.		

You should have answered yes to each item in the checklist. Work toward correcting any negative answers.

ORGANIZING YOUR PRESENTATION

A well-organized presentation shows in the implementation. Position key points in strategic places, and keep everything in logical order to allow people to follow easily. If your audience cannot follow your logic, you will lose them. Be absolutely clear.

Ideas must be presented coherently and consistently if the audience is to believe you know the material well. Rearrange the order of your presentation if there is any doubt about the sequence of information.

Scattered thoughts sabotage a presentation. You do not want listeners to feel as if they walked in on the middle of your presentation.

Jot down a few words pertaining to each idea on individual index cards to jog your memory throughout the presentation. Avoid writing out your entire speech on the cards. Number the index cards so you will be able to rearrange them if they become out of order.

Organize handouts and visual aids in the order in which you will need them to avoid shuffling through them to find the right one at a particular point in your presentation. (Handouts and visual aids are covered in detail in Chapter 3, "Developing Visual Aids.")

A good way to organize your entire presentation is by using a binder with plastic sleeves. Store together in the same plastic sleeve the individual note cards and specific handouts or hard copies of visuals that go together. Note cards that do not have matching visuals or handouts can be stored by themselves in individual sleeves. Arrange the material in the order in which you intend to present it. All handouts, note cards, and hard copies of visuals can be stored in the binder. Add anything else that pertains to your presentation, such as flash drives.

Complete the following checklist.

Checklist for Effective Organizing	Yes	No
I have organized everything I need for my presentation in a binder.		
I have decided on the relevant points to present.		
I have written out my speech in a logical order.		
I have sufficient information to support my key points.		
I have prepared note cards to aid my memory.		
I have organized visual aids and handouts in the order in which I will use them.		
I have appropriate examples, stories, or anecdotes to use during the presentation.		
I have a takeaway for the audience.		
I have determined how I want my audience to act or react after my presentation and organized my presentation to that end.		

You should have answered yes to each item in the checklist. Work toward correcting any negative answers.

Exercise: Organize Your Presentation

The next time you are called upon to give a presentation, complete the following exercise.

Presentation topic _____

Sources for research notes

_____

_____

_____

_____

_____

_____

_____

_____

_____

Key points to cover

1. _____

_____

_____

_____

_____

_____

2. _____

_____

_____

_____

_____

_____

3. _____

_____

_____

_____

_____

Anecdotes or examples I plan to use

_____

_____

_____

_____

_____

_____

Supporting information for key points

_____

_____

_____

_____

_____

_____

Visual aids I plan to use

_____

_____

_____

_____

_____

_____

Handouts I plan to use

_____

_____

_____

_____

The takeaway for my audience

_____

_____

_____

_____

_____

_____

_____

The reaction I hope to elicit from my audience

_____

_____

_____

_____

_____

_____

_____

CHAPTER 2

Writing the Text

Write (or key) the text of your talk regardless of whether you are presenting informally or formally. Great speakers make presenting information seem effortless, but that is rarely the case. Advanced preparation and planning, including writing out the text of the talk and practicing the speech, are keys to success.

Assembling your presentation will be easier once you have planned using the suggestions in Chapter 1, "Planning and Organizing." Begin thinking about the text of your presentation by becoming thoroughly familiar with your topic and what is expected of you as a speaker. If you have not done so, complete the appropriate exercises in Chapter 1, particularly the form for brainstorming and choosing key ideas. You may also want to outline your talk under the headings Introduction, Main Body, and Conclusion.

DEFINE YOUR TOPIC

If you have been assigned a topic or subject area, be sure you are clear about what the event organizers (or whoever asked you to present) want from you. If you have not been given a topic or specifics about a subject area, decide on a topic best suited to your audience. If need be, run your topic past the organizers to ensure it is acceptable.

Focus on the topic and keep reinforcing it throughout your presentation.

CHOOSE A FEW KEY POINTS

After determining the central theme of your presentation, choose a few key points to support the topic, as discussed in Chapter 1. You may have a lot to cover, but you cannot hold your audience's attention for hours on end. Focus on what is important to them.

How do you decide what to include in your presentation? Base everything on your topic and purpose. From that, decide why this specific audience came to hear you speak. Ask yourself, "What is the most important thing for my audience to know?" Repeat the question, asking what is the second (and third and fourth) thing that is important for your audience to know.

Key points should include information you were asked to deliver as well as information you feel is crucial to understanding your subject. Always provide correct, relevant, up-to-date information.

Keep key points to a minimum. You will not want to overwhelm your audience, confuse them, or cause them to cease listening to you. If you deliver excessive points you refer to as key material, it devalues the overall information. Listeners may lose sight of what specifically they should remember. Naturally, you will be presenting what you consider to be important information throughout the presentation, but *key* indicates that particular fact is central to the entire talk. Capture the essence of your talk in three to five points.

Arrange your key points in a logical sequence, and then fully discuss one point before moving on to another. Talk about all supporting information and materials that belong with a particular point when discussing it.

Exercise: Choose Key Points for Your Presentation

When you are next called upon to give a presentation, write down three to five key points to cover along with the information you will use to support each point.

1. Key point _____

   _____

   Supporting information _____

   _____

   _____

2. Key point _____

_____

Supporting information _____

_____

_____

_____

3. Key point _____

_____

Supporting information _____

_____

_____

_____

4. Key point _____

_____

Supporting information _____

_____

_____

_____

5. Key point _____

_____

Supporting information _____

_____

_____

_____

STRUCTURE YOUR PRESENTATION

How can you best engage your audience? By considering your particular topic and your specific audience, you can develop an interesting presentation. Not all information lends itself to the same type of presentation or to the same group of people. For instance, slides of animal pictures might be appropriate for animal lovers, the local zoo employees, or children. However, those slides would not be appropriate for the CEOs of companies. The same is true for content. A serious subject would be treated differently from a lighthearted theme complete with joking and laughing. Tailor the presentation and your delivery to the topic and audience. (Additional information on tailoring a presentation is detailed later in this chapter and in Chapter 6, "Focusing on Your Audience.")

All presentations are structured with an introduction, middle (body of the talk), and conclusion. However, what is included in each section and how the information in those sections is arranged may differ.

Ask yourself the following questions to determine an appropriate structure for your presentation.

- ✦ What is your topic, and have you thoroughly researched it?
- ✦ What format would best suit your audience (straight lecture, discussion, hands-on or other type of audience participation, and so on)?
- ✦ Will you use visual aids?
- ✦ Will you use examples, samples, or stories?
- ✦ Will you present in a formal or informal setting?
- ✦ How much time will you devote to the introduction, the main body, and the conclusion?
- ✦ Will you have a question-and-answer session following the presentation?
- ✦ Will the audience be able to interact with you during the presentation (questions, discussion, exercises, and so on)?
- ✦ What will the audience gain from, learn from, or do with the material presented?

Once you create a central topic, you can branch out from there and decide how many key points are necessary and what approach you should take to delivering them.

Introduction

Use the introduction to capture your audience's attention. If you do not grab the audience members' attention with your opening sentences, you will have a difficult or impossible time getting them to concentrate on the rest of the presentation.

Begin by connecting with the audience. If you have not been introduced by a host, introduce yourself and give a brief bio. Describe your background and why it qualifies you to present. If you have something in common with the audience, mention it. Keep your introduction brief.

How can you best relate to the audience? Make it personal by building rapport with your listeners through openers that include anecdotes, questions, statistics, personal experiences, relevant stories, or appropriate jokes personalized for them. Show the audience you have something in common with them.

Introduce your topic by telling the audience what you are going to talk about during the presentation. Let them know exactly what they can expect to hear and how they will benefit by listening to you.

Example for the Introduction of a Stress Management Presentation

Stress affects all of us. Today's presentation will focus on how you can live a healthier life by controlling your stress through proven techniques. Stress can be positive or negative, and its effects can be mentally or physically damaging. I will talk about the types of stress you might encounter as well as its causes. I will discuss the effects stress has on the body and mind and then suggest possible ways for managing it.

Middle

Use the middle of your presentation to deliver the substance of your topic. Your entire talk should be developed around this message. Introduce key points, and keep reminding the audience of the benefits of your message to them.

Stick to your topic. If you do not deliver the talk people came to hear, they may walk away disappointed and irritated. Provide information in a logical format, emphasizing the most important facts. Tailor your talk to the audience, using appropriate terminology and examples. If you can relate your talk to what the audience already knows, they may have an easier time grasping the concept.

Check your facts for accuracy, and have sufficient supporting evidence to defend your key points. Provide up-to-date, well-researched information and, if applicable, visuals and handouts that complement your talk. You may want to have a few questions on hand to ask your audience throughout the presentation to spark their interest and keep them attentive. Providing an opportunity for the audience to text questions to be answered at the end of a presentation is a great way to involve a younger audience.

Although the middle of your talk comprises the majority of your presentation, keep your message clear and brief. You will lose your audience with a long, boring speech that makes it difficult for them to focus. Pace yourself so you do not run over the allotted time. Allow sufficient time for a question-and-answer session.

Example for the Body of a Stress Management Presentation

I will now discuss the effects stress has on the body mentally and physically, give reasons for wanting to control your stress, and provide a number of tips for managing stress. (The speaker should then proceed to discuss this information in detail and use visuals if appropriate.)

Conclusion

Be conscious of your time and know when to stop talking. Allow time to summarize your presentation and reiterate key points. Tie everything together, and let your audience know what you expect them to do when you finish your presentation—buy a product, solve a problem, feel motivated, and so forth. Draw a strong conclusion that will inspire your audience to take the action you prefer. Provide an appropriate recap of the talk. Tell your audience what action you want them to take.

Make the conclusion satisfying for the audience by telling them what they learned or what they gained by listening to you.

Example of the Conclusion of a Stress Management Presentation

To recap what we've learned, you can alleviate stress by doing the following: (Here the speaker should reiterate a few top stress-busting techniques he talked about in the presentation.)

Question-and-Answer Period

Welcome questions from a participating audience. If time and format permit, take questions during the presentation. When fitting, add a question-and-answer period at the end of your talk. Be sure to allow enough time during the planning stage of your presentation to accommodate the questions and your response to them.

Listen attentively to questions and comments to be certain you understand what is being asked. If you are not clear, ask for clarification. Repeat the question before you give your answer so everyone can hear it.

Answer questions thoroughly, but relevantly, by focusing on the specific question asked. Do not go off on a tangent unrelated to the question. The question-and-answer period is not the time to continue your lecture, but an opportunity to clarify a question in a listener's mind. Rambling will not only confuse the person asking but also the audience.

If you do not know the answer to a question, be honest. Offer to find out the answer if possible. By thoroughly researching your topic before the presentation and gathering more facts than you need, you will likely have sufficient information to answer a variety of questions. Remember, you are the expert on the subject.

Complete the following checklist.

Checklist for Structuring Your Presentation	Yes	No
Is your topic clear?		
Have you researched enough information to support your presentation?		
Do you have an attention-grabbing opener?		
Have you prepared three to five key points for the main body of your talk?		
Do you have sufficient, viable information related to your key points to sustain your presentation?		
Is your information presented in a logical order?		
Do you have sufficient sources and information to support your main points?		
Have you prepared appropriate visuals, examples, samples, and so on?		
Did you plan for interaction with the audience?		
Did you allow time for a question-and-answer discussion?		
Do you have a strong conclusion that will encourage your audience to take appropriate action?		
Does your conclusion summarize what the audience has learned?		
Does your conclusion include the takeaway for the audience?		
Is your conclusion likely to get the audience to act or react the way you desire?		

You should have answered yes to each item in the checklist. Work toward correcting any negative answers.

USE APPROPRIATE WORDS AND LANGUAGE

Select the appropriate words for your particular audience. (Chapter 6 details audience focus.) For instance, language appropriate for an adult may not be understood by elementary students. Technical terms suitable for colleagues in your field may not be fully understood by the general public. Avoid jargon and technical words that may be unfamiliar to your audience. Use easy-to-understand words and uncomplicated sentences.

To be convincing and have a positive effect on your audience, avoid negative words and statements. Instead of telling the audience what *not* to do, tell them what they *should* do. Rather than say, "Do not eat unhealthy foods," say, "Eat healthy foods." Instead of saying, "I'm not sure," try, "I will find out for you." Turn "I can't" into "Here's what I can do."

If you are trying to persuade your audience or move them to take action, use direct language so they know exactly what you mean and what you expect of them. If you have a request, ask. If you want listeners to buy your products, tell them. If you want your department to increase sales, advise them of the percentage or amount of growth you expect, and then explain how to accomplish the task. Some speakers talk all around their requests but never quite tell people what they should do. Ask if people understand what they should do and how to do it or if they need clarification.

Eliminate slang and poor speech habits such as saying, "ah," "um," "you know," and the like, which detract from your message and performance. Speak proper grammar, and work at increasing your vocabulary. Speakers with an excellent command of language have a greater impact on their listeners. However, take care not to speak above your listener's understanding. If they need a dictionary to interpret your words, people will stop listening. Check your pronunciations, especially with proper names.

Be mindful of audience members who are not proficient in the language you speak. If you will be speaking to an international audience, you will have to research the language and customs of that country and perhaps arrange for an interpreter.

Write out a succinct, clear message based on your key points, and practice speaking it out loud.

Exercise: Structure Your Presentation

Complete the following exercise when you want to plan your next presentation.

Presentation topic _____

Introduction: Attention grabber (anecdote, question, statistic, joke, and so on) _____

_____

_____

_____

_____

_____

Middle: Key points to cover

1. _____

_____

_____

_____

_____

_____

_____

2. _____

_____

_____

_____

_____

_____

_____

_____

3. _____

_____

_____

_____

_____

_____

_____

4. _____

_____

_____

_____

_____

_____

_____

5. _____

_____

_____

_____

_____

_____

Conclusion: Reiterate key points and call audience to action _____

_____

_____

_____

_____

_____

_____

_____

_____

_____

_____

TAILOR YOUR PRESENTATION

Your audience is the main consideration for your presentation. Aim to please your audience by tailoring your presentation to those individuals. What worked in a former speech may or may not work again, depending on the audience. For instance, a stress management presentation for a group of daycare workers would have a different spin than one for a group of financial advisors. Although the basic information might be the same, these two very different audiences would be looking for specific help for their particular situations. Daycare workers may want to know how to keep calm around screaming, crying children. The financial advisors may want to know how to relax after dealing with disgruntled clients all day. Use examples and visuals that relate to the specific audience you are addressing. Begin planning early so you are not rushed or tempted to recycle old material that does not suit.

Ask yourself:

- ✦ What is the purpose of my presentation?
- ✦ What will I communicate?
- ✦ Who is my audience?

- ✦ Will my message be of interest to this audience?
- ✦ How can I tailor my message for this event?
- ✦ Can I build on what the audience knows about my topic?
- ✦ What questions or exercises would get my audience involved in the presentation?
- ✦ How will I approach this presentation?
- ✦ What examples and visuals would fit this specific presentation?
- ✦ Am I using easy-to-understand language for this presentation?
- ✦ Is my language positive?
- ✦ Have I limited my ideas to a few key points geared to this presentation?
- ✦ What action do I want my audience to take?
- ✦ If I am using notes from a former presentation, how can I tailor them to this particular talk?
- ✦ How can I update my notes and visual aids, including handouts, to fit this presentation?

Another consideration is the size of the audience and the venue. Speaking to an informal group of three or four in an office or conference room is different from addressing an audience of hundreds in a convention center. Also, formal meetings call for a different approach than informal ones.

Ask yourself these questions:

- ✦ How large is my audience?
- ✦ What is the setting for the presentation?
- ✦ Is this a formal or informal presentation?

Complete the following checklist.

Checklist for Tailoring My Presentation	Yes	No
What is the purpose of my presentation?		
Have I tailored my presentation for this particular speech and event?		
Will my audience understand my topic?		
Can I build on what my audience knows about my subject?		
Can I build and maintain interest in my presentation?		
Did I factor in ways to involve my audience in my presentation?		
Do I know specifically what I want my audience to take away from this presentation?		
Do I have questions and examples for this particular presentation?		
Have I used easy-to-understand language?		
Have I considered the different learning styles of my audience?		

Checklist for Tailoring My Presentation	Yes	No
Is my information credible?		
Have I thought about appealing visuals for this particular presentation?		
Is my language appropriate for this audience?		
Is my language positive?		
If I am using notes and visuals from former presentations, have I updated them?		

You should have answered yes to each item in the checklist. Work toward correcting any negative answers.

Exercise: Tailor a Presentation

Plan your next presentation by completing the following:

Topic _____

What is the purpose of this presentation? _____

_____

_____

_____

_____

_____

_____

What can I do to build this presentation around the audience's knowledge of this topic? _____

_____

_____

_____

_____

_____

_____

Have I used language my audience can relate to and understand? _____

Will my audience be receptive to my information and the way it is presented? _____

Have I constructed my presentation in a way that fits this particular event and venue? _____

What stories and exercises will I use to construct an interesting presentation? _____

_____

_____

_____

_____

_____

How will I approach this presentation (lecture, visuals, hands-on, and so on)? _____

_____

_____

_____

These are the main points to remember about this presentation.

_____

_____

_____

_____

_____

_____

What visual aids are best suited to this presentation? _____

_____

_____

_____

_____

_____

_____

What handouts are best suited to this presentation? _____

_____

_____

_____

_____

CHAPTER 3

Developing Visual Aids

Once you have written the text of your talk, you may need to work on supplemental materials such as handouts and visual aids to help the audience understand your intended message and learn from it. Visual aids impact a presentation. High-quality visuals strengthen the presentation, and poor-quality ones weaken it. To ensure that your visual aids complement your talk and don't detract from it, aim for aesthetically appealing, well-designed visuals.

Too many visuals and handouts will overwhelm your audience. After all, the audience came to hear you talk, not to hear you read from your handouts or visuals. When deciding how many visuals you will need and what to include on them, consider the type of information you want to communicate. Complex information, graphics, and figures are best conveyed through handouts and other visuals. Demonstrations may require instructional handouts, videos, slides, equipment, and products. Application practice and training exercises lend themselves to handouts, videos, equipment, and devices.

Keep a backup of your handouts, slides, and videos in a separate location such as the cloud or a flash drive.

HANDOUTS/WORKSHEETS

Most people who attend presentations appreciate handouts or some other takeaway they can later review to refresh their memories. In addition, many people are visual learners who appreciate the opportunity to follow along in a visual format as the speaker presents information.

Handouts can be successful tools for involving your audience in the presentation. You can prepare handouts the participants will fill out or with an exercise for them to complete, or you can leave room for them to take notes as they follow the talk.

Create relevant handouts that clearly and succinctly summarize the information you present. You may have a wealth of information to pass along, but unless you are giving participants a book to take home and read, you will want to limit the number of handouts. Keep your audience and their specific needs in mind.

Use easy-to-read fonts and colors, and arrange information in an attractive format. Do not overdo bullets and numbering, all caps, bold, and underline. Software programs that offer a variety of embellishments, images, and WordArt create the temptation to generate outlandish documents. For professional-looking materials, avoid fancy, extraneous enhancements.

After making copies of the handouts for your audience, check that they are clear and clean of smudges. The timing of the distribution of handouts can be tricky. The best procedure is to distribute the handouts when the audience will need to use them. If you distribute handouts that include most of your speech or that are lengthy, your audience may spend more time reading than listening to you. If your audience needs to consult the information on the handouts during your talk or must complete an exercise, distribute those handouts at the beginning of the talk or another appropriate time. If handouts are merely references to be used later, distribute them at the end of your presentation. Your personal copies of handouts will make convenient references during your presentation.

Delivering handouts electronically can be a convenience for you and for traveling attendees. They also provide a backup plan if you run out of hard copies. With an electronic backup, let the audience know you will email handouts to those who contact you through your email. It is a good idea to have a line at the bottom of your handouts citing sources and your contact information, including email and website addresses.

Determine if handouts need to be updated each time you use them for a different presentation. Is the information still current? Use only those handouts that will supplement the particular talk you are giving.

Complete the following checklist.

Checklist for Preparing Handouts	Yes	No
Are my handouts essential to my presentation?		
Did I use easy-to-read fonts?		
Did I use a limited amount of easy-to-read colors?		
Have I limited bullets and other embellishments?		
Have I tailored my handouts to this particular presentation?		
Is my audience likely to benefit from my handouts?		

Checklist for Preparing Handouts	Yes	No
Have I limited the number of different handouts I am distributing?		
Is the information on my handouts credible?		
Have I credited my sources when necessary?		
Have I made enough copies of the handouts?		
Are copies of my handouts clean and legible?		
Have I made backup copies of my handouts?		

You should have answered yes to each item in the checklist. Work toward correcting any negative answers.

Exercise: Assess Your Handouts

For your next presentation, analyze the handouts you create by completing the following:

How will this handout complement the presentation?

_____

_____

_____

_____

_____

_____

_____

Describe the visual appeal of the handout, including text, graphics, fonts, embellishments, and the like.

_____

_____

_____

_____

_____

_____

_____

Have you limited the text to essential information? _____

Is the handout information credible? _____

Have your cited sources you used to create the handout? _____

Have you tailored the handout to your presentation? _____

If you are reusing handouts from a previous presentation, have you updated them? _____

Are you relying on reading the handouts to get you through your presentation? _____

Have you limited the number of handouts? _____

Have you made a backup copy of your handouts? _____

VISUALS: SLIDES

Most presenters use slides or other visuals, especially when they are giving lengthy talks. The right visual aids will enhance your presentation. Visuals should be relevant, easy to read, and easy to understand.

Software programs such as PowerPoint and Keynote make it easy to create slides. However, it is just as easy to create poor-quality slides as it is to create superior-quality ones. It all depends on the designer. Some presenters get carried away creating elaborate visuals that have too much text, a mix of fancy fonts, garish embellishments, a rainbow of colors, and tedious graphics. These visuals can be boring and distracting for the audience.

Visuals should enhance your presentation, not take the place of your talk. Plan the slides around what you have to say by using them to add images to your words. Limit the number of slides.

The best slides are the ones viewers can interpret and understand at a glance and that are pleasing to the eye. Do not cram lists or paragraphs on the slide, filling up all the blank space. The current trend is not to clutter the slides with bullets and irrelevant graphics. Less is more when it comes to slides. Proofread your text carefully.

Use key words and phrases that you can expand on as you talk. If you place your entire talk on slides, you may be tempted to read from the slide instead of interacting with your audience. Slides should be used to help the audience understand your message, not for you to read your speech. A slide is handy for jogging your memory should you forget something, but you should not use it as a crutch or because you are ill prepared.

Avoid templates, because they could make your presentation look amateurish. Many of them have a manufactured look, and the more extravagant, garish ones can be off putting. Plain backgrounds are preferred, not fancy ones.

Be Sensible with Fonts

Restraint when choosing fonts is a must. What looks good on your computer may not look presentable or readable on the screen. In addition, the fonts you chose may not be installed on the computer you will be using for your presentation, causing your fonts to default to an unflattering style. Choose standard font styles in simple sans serif types that are compatible with most equipment.

Sans serif means the letters have no embellishments at the ends of the letters, such as swirls or dots. Arial is a common sans serif font. Times Roman is a common serif font. Avoid WordArt, italics, unusual symbols, and decorative fonts on slides. They may be difficult to read from the screen.

Do not mix and match a variety of fonts. Stick to one or two throughout the presentation. Avoid keying in all caps, because it is considered a form of yelling. Standard uppercase and lowercase rules should be applied.

Choose a font size that your audience can easily see from the screen at a distance. Create titles in 36 to 48 point and the text body in at least 24 point.

Use Color Effectively

Text color depends on background color. Light text works well on dark backgrounds, and dark text works best on light backgrounds. If text color is too bright or is a pastel color, it may be difficult to read from the screen, especially when there is a glare.

Color can be used to call attention to important points, but too many colors make a slide look busy. Use only one or two colors for text. Of course, images and graphics can be more colorful as long as they are not distracting.

Applying a color theme will give your slides consistency throughout. A color theme is a combination of matching shades of the same colors that complement one another. Professional-looking colors are blues, greens, grays, and the like.

Include Images to Reinforce Your Point

Software programs make it easy to embed images and graphics into slides. An image or two on each slide will give your audience a way to pull the presentation information together. Keep images to a minimum, however, so as not to confuse or distract people. Aim for balance between text and images and a clean, uncomplicated appearance.

Today you can find images everywhere—in magazines and journals, in books and newspapers, on Internet sites, in brochures and advertising packets, and even in your company's materials. Invest the time to find high-quality images and graphics that supplement your talk.

Make sure your images are not copyrighted before copying or scanning them into your slides and other visuals, or give credit for using them.

Your software program may include clip art, but do not use it in slides if you are aiming to impress; they have become overused, and most people are familiar with them. Free and cheap images and graphics are not recommended either for professional presentations. Clip art and poor-quality images have a tendency to make your visuals look amateurish and make you seem technologically challenged.

You can find royalty-free stock images online, but take note that some are expensive and of poor quality. Try Google Images, Instagram, Slide Share, and Pinterest, as well as general Internet sites. Choose images that clearly enhance your speech and that have a professional appearance.

If you have a good digital camera or high-quality camera on your cell phone, you can take your own pictures and upload them to your computer for insertion into slides. Make sure the camera is high resolution and takes clear, high-grade pictures. Again, be sure not to infringe on copyrighted material. To protect your interests, you may need to obtain a written release from individuals who are subjects in your slides. You can also buy computer art on CDs in computer stores and online.

If you are artistic, you might use one of the drawing software programs to create your own unique designs and images.

Animation is not recommended for most professional business presentations, but you can use it to transition between slides or add interest in informal presentations.

You can embed tables and graphs into slides, but they should be simple and uncluttered to be effective. Check the table format if you type it in one program and then transfer it to another. Sometimes switching to a different program will cause your table and its contents to go askew.

Make a hard copy of your slides for yourself and, if appropriate, for your audience. Create a backup copy and store it elsewhere.

Tips for Slides

- Limit the number of fonts; choose a sans serif font style.
- Limit the number of colors; use a color theme.
- Limit the text.
- Choose an easy-to-read font point size.
- Use only high-quality photos, images, and graphics.
- Avoid fancy embellishments and bullets.
- Analyze high-quality slides, and replicate similar ones.
- Analyze your slides.
- Avoid reading your speech from slides.
- Print a hard copy set of the slides.
- Make backup copies of your slides.

Refresh Tired Slides

If your slides and other visuals are years old, it may be time for a facelift. Eliminate old-fashioned, overdone colors and styles for PowerPoint presentations. Where bullets, clip art, and lots of text were once the norm, they are scarce today. Modern slides have a crisp, clean look with a few key words or lines of text and superior images and graphics.

Search the Internet for slides and visuals. Look through a significant number of them to see what is new and what looks outdated. Take particular note of the visuals when you attend presentations. Check to see what your company is using in its marketing and advertising materials. Look through journals and magazines. Watch television ads and look at billboards. Take webinars. If you have friends in the marketing or advertising field, consult them on your visuals and ask for recommendations or improvements.

Analyze the visuals you researched to determine which are the most appealing. Emulate those that appeal to you and fit your presentation. Choose slides that are superior in quality.

Investing the time to research and create outstanding visuals will have a big payoff in the delivery of your presentation. Terrific visuals have the potential to engage and excite your audience.

Practice with Your Visuals

Once you have created your visuals, practice using them with your speech. Become so familiar with what is on the visuals that you are not tempted to read from them. If possible, practice your visuals on the equipment you will use during your actual presentation to avoid surprises such as the visuals being difficult to read or being incompatible with the computer at the location where you are presenting.

Preferably, practice in front of people. If you cannot find someone to practice in front of, run through the presentation on your own out loud in front of a mirror.

Proofread Your Slides

Read every word of every slide carefully. You will not want a glaring error to be displayed on the screen for all to see. Check your spelling and grammar.

Make sure you have covered all the important points but have not overused text. Analyze the overall appearance of the slides. Have a friend or an associate read and review the slides.

Complete the following checklist.

Checklist for Preparing Visual Aids and Handouts	Yes	No
Are my visual aids clear and easy to read?		
Have I limited text on my visuals?		
Have I used easy-to-read fonts and colors?		
Have I used high-quality images and graphics?		
Have I tailored my visuals to this particular audience?		
Am I using only enough visuals to get the message across?		
Will my visuals add to my presentation in a positive way?		
Have I considered the different learning styles of my audience?		
Is the information on my visuals credible?		
Have I credited my sources when necessary?		
Have I refreshed any visuals I used in the past?		
Have I carefully proofread the visuals?		
Are my copies clean and legible?		
Have I made copies of the visuals for myself?		
Did I make backup copies of my work?		

You should have answered yes to each item in the checklist. Work toward correcting any negative answers.

Exercise: Research and Analyze Slides

Search various Internet sites for slides. Study the graphics and photos. Analyze each slide by describing the following:

Describe the visual attractiveness and appeal of the slide.

_____

_____

_____

_____

_____

Describe the use of graphics and images.

_____

_____

_____

_____

_____

Describe the appeal of the fonts and color.

_____

_____

_____

_____

_____

Describe the use of bullets and other embellishments.

_____

_____

_____

_____

_____

Exercise: Create and Analyze Slides

Analyze each slide you create for your next presentation by completing the following:

How will this slide complement the presentation?

_____

_____

_____

_____

_____

_____

Describe the visual appeal of the slide, including text, graphics, pictures and images, fonts, embellishments, and the like.

_____

_____

_____

_____

_____

_____

Have you limited the text on the slide? _____

Is the information on the slide credible? _____

Have you cited sources you used to create the slide? _____

Have you tailored the slide to your presentation? _____

Does the slide add value to the presentation? _____

Have you carefully proofread each slide? _____

If you are reusing visuals from a previous presentation, have you updated them? _____

Are you relying on reading the slide to get you through your presentation? _____

Do you have an appropriate number of slides? _____

Have you copied a set of slides for yourself and for your audience (if appropriate)? _____

Have you made a backup copy of your slides? _____

VIDEOS AND AUDIOVISUALS

Videos should be professionally created or at the very least have a professional look and sound if you prepared them yourself. For videos in which you are the subject, prepare what you want to say and practice several times before the performance is recorded. Use quality recording equipment. Limit the information on the video to what is advantageous to your presentation. When other individuals are filmed in the videos you plan to show to the public, obtain written permission from them.

If you are showing a prerecorded video related to your subject matter, preview it beforehand and time it with your entire presentation.

Audiovisuals should be professionally recorded. They must be created with a pleasant-sounding voice that is free of accents, quirks, careless habits, and incorrect pronunciations.

MISCELLANEOUS VISUAL AIDS

Some presentations lend themselves to other types of visual aids, such as equipment, clothing, merchandise and other goods. Check the safety, appeal, and visual appearance of all display and demonstration aids. Make sure equipment and products with moveable parts are working properly.

Exercise: Practice Your Presentation with Your Visuals

Practice your next presentation from beginning to end using your slides, videos, and other visuals. Analyze how well the visuals complement the speech.

PART II

Facilities

CHAPTER 4

Learning About the Venue, Room Layout, and Amenities

This chapter deals with the venue in which you will be speaking. It does not provide information for organizing the event and venue; rather the tips are meant for the presenter. Get to know the venue and room layout so you will be in a better position to execute your presentation.

Answer these questions when asked to speak:

✦ In what type of setting will I be presenting?

✦ Am I meeting one-on-one with an individual?

✦ Am I attending a typical business meeting?

✦ Am I meeting a small group in an informal setting?

✦ Am I presenting to a large audience in a formal setting?

✦ Can you describe the room?

✦ Will I have a podium and microphone?

✦ Will I have access to audio visual equipment?

✦ Do I have any input as to the venue?

The answers to these questions will help you determine how and what to prepare.

INDIVIDUAL AND SMALL GROUP MEETINGS

If you are meeting with an individual, you will not need a podium and microphone. If you know the individual's preference as to venue, you can relate to him in a way with which he is most comfortable. You could meet over lunch or in an office. If he is a visual learner, you can show him pictures, slides, videos, or handouts to get your message across. You are more likely to be relaxed during a one-on-one talk, depending on the circumstances, than a formal presentation.

Small group meetings can be informal or formal, depending on the topic and venue. If you have input concerning the venue, choose a location where you would be most comfortable. Depending on your presentation, secure the equipment and materials you will need.

FORMAL PRESENTATIONS

Formal presentations require quite a bit of planning. Many times you will not have a choice when it comes to the venue for your speech. If you are attending a convention or formal event, the organizers will make the arrangements, and you will not be consulted about their decisions. However, you may be able to ask for things that will make your presentation proceed smoothly. For example, when you prefer to use a projector versus a laptop, ask if a projector is available. If you prefer a walk-around mic instead of a podium-mounted microphone, ask for one. If you prefer to stand behind the audience and operate audiovisual equipment, check the room layout to see if it works for you. Try to make your presentation venue as comfortable for you as possible by petitioning the organizers for minor allowances that make a major difference.

When presenting in an unfamiliar setting, you may want to arrive at the event early enough to check the layout of the room and to make sure the proper equipment you will need is on hand and working.

Layout

If you are speaking to a large group, the room arrangement may be important to your presentation. For this particular presentation, answer these questions:

✦ Do you prefer a podium at the front of the room with the audience facing you sitting in chairs?

✦ Do you prefer to stand behind the audience while they view a screen as you explain?

✦ From its current location, can the screen be seen by everyone in the room?

✦ Do you need the audience to have desks on which to write?

✦ Do you prefer to have chairs or desks arranged in rows?

✦ Do you prefer a more intimate arrangement of chairs, such as a large or small semicircle?

✦ Are the audience chairs comfortable?

✦ Will participants be working in small groups at tables arranged accordingly?

✦ Is the lighting sufficient?

✦ Does the sun or lighting create a glare on your visuals?

✦ Is the room a comfortable temperature?

✦ Is the room clean and neat?

- ◆ Are there enough outlets in the room?
- ◆ Is water provided for the presenter and for the audience?
- ◆ How are the acoustics?
- ◆ Is there sufficient room to comfortably seat the number of participants you expect?
- ◆ Do you know to whom you should speak if you need something before or during your presentation?

Be sure you have adequate space, sufficient lighting, a comfortable atmosphere, a clean area, and a room arrangement that suits your particular presentation. If you will have difficulty presenting in the current setup, your audience will have trouble focusing. Crowded, hot, uncomfortable audiences that have difficulty seeing and hearing you as the presenter will get little but irritation out of the event.

Find out who handles problems as they arise during the event you are attending. How should you contact that person if you need assistance before or during your presentation?

Complete the following checklist after viewing the room for your presentation.

Checklist for Room Layout	Yes	No
Is the arrangement conducive to my presentation?		
Is the lighting sufficient?		
Is the room a comfortable temperature?		
Are the chairs comfortable and arranged the way I prefer (semicircle or straight rows)?		
Do participants have a writing surface if they need one?		
Is the room sufficient to hold the number of participants expected?		
Do I have a podium and microphone if I need them?		
Do I have the audiovisual equipment I need?		
Can the screen be viewed from all the seats?		
Do I know how to operate the microphone and audiovisual equipment?		
Are there enough electrical outlets in the room?		
Do I have water at the podium?		
Is the room clean and neat?		
Do I know whom to contact if I have a problem?		

You should have answered yes to each item in the checklist. Work toward correcting any negative answers.

Microphones

Speaking with a microphone can be tricky if you have not been properly instructed. The main issue is standing the correct distance from the microphone—too close, and a whistling sound might accompany your words, but too far away, and you will not be heard.

If the microphone is mounted on a podium, stand so your mouth is a few inches away from it. You can usually adjust the microphone up and down. Face the microphone at all times. When you turn your head, your voice will not project.

Hand-held microphones are convenient for presenters who prefer to move around while talking and for those who want to engage their audiences by holding the microphone up to the individual audience members and allowing them to speak.

As the name implies, lapel mics are clipped to your lapel. This allows you to move around hands-free while you are speaking.

Remember that everything you say and the noises you make will be projected over the microphone. Be conscious of making inadvertent comments, clearing your throat, or making distracting noises.

Whatever microphone style you are using, ask the audience if everyone can hear you, especially those in the back of the room.

Know the procedure to follow if you have a problem with the microphone.

Miscellaneous Tools and Amenities

Assorted amenities provide comfort and convenience for the presenter. If you need additional items other than those provided, ask the event organizer if it is possible to obtain them. Examples of such amenities are listed next.

CONVENIENCES

As a presenter, you will want to have water during your talk. Some venues provide water and refreshment stations in or near the event room. Conventions and conferences may include lunch or dinner.

PODIUMS

Podiums come in a variety of styles and designs. They are convenient for storing notes, handouts, and a glass of water but present a problem for people who like to lean against things. Stand straight at a slight distance from the podium, but close enough to be heard over a podium-mounted microphone.

FLIP CHARTS

Flip charts are useful for small, informal meetings. You can use them to convey small bits of information (sales figures, product information, lists, and so on) or to brainstorm ideas. If you make notes on the flip chart before the presentation, you can use those notes to focus the audience's attention and to jog your memory as your speak. Be sure to have several working felt-tip markers on hand to write your points. Writing in different colors can effectively highlight information, but too many colors can be confusing to the audience. Stand to the side of the chart while writing so your audience can see your work. When finished with the pages, you can save them for another presentation or display them for the participants.

ELECTRONIC WHITE BOARDS

You can use electronic white boards the same way as flip charts, except you have to erase the information as you move through your presentation. Some electronic boards have the capability to make copies of what is written on them. Have several working dry-erase markers and an eraser on hand.

PROJECTORS

Although an older form of technology, projectors are still in use. Ask for explicit instructions if you are unfamiliar with this equipment. It is important to focus the lens properly and aim the projector correctly. Stand to the side so you don't block the screen.

TECHNICAL PROBLEMS

You may have created exceptional slides, but if your program is not compatible with the equipment you will be using at the venue, the look of your slides could be spoiled. For instance, if you use a font that is not on the PC or Mac you will be presenting from, your text will be affected, possibly in size and format.

A new version of a program you created your slides in may be on the laptop at the venue, and this will affect your presentation. Also, if your version of software differs from that of the venue's equipment, you may encounter a problem. If you used a lower version program, a higher version program can read it. However, if you used a higher version program, a lower version program cannot read it. One thing you can do is save your work in a lower version program as well as the one in which you are working. If you created your slides on a PC and will present them on a Mac, the entire layout of the slide may be skewed.

If possible, use a PC to present if you created slides on a PC, and use a Mac if you created slides on a Mac. Practice your presentation, including the slides, on the equipment you will be using to ensure a smooth delivery. The best case scenario is to use your own laptop both for creating and delivering the material.

Save your work on the cloud or a flash drive in case you encounter an equipment problem or the loss or corruption of your work. Always have backups.

Learn who handles technical problems for the venue and how to contact that person during the event. Ask the organizers these questions:

✦ Who handles technical problems?

✦ Who handles problems with the room (the microphone, the seating arrangement, the temperature, the lighting, and so on)?

✦ How do I contact the proper person if I need assistance?

✦ Who can show me how to operate the audiovisual equipment?

Exercise: Critique the Venue

The next time you are called on to give a presentation to a large group, learn as much as you can about the venue by answering the following questions:

Type of event and venue _____

_____

Size of audience _____

Are the accommodations sufficient for the number of attendees? _____

Layout of the room (chairs or desks and arrangement of the furniture) _____

_____

_____

What kind of audiovisual equipment will I need? _____

_____

_____

_____

Will I need a podium? _____

Will I need a microphone? If so, what type do I prefer? _____

_____

Are desks or chairs arranged in a manner conducive to my presentation? If not, what can I do about it?

_____

_____

_____

Is the lighting sufficient? If not, how can it be improved? _____

_____

_____

_____

Is the room a comfortable temperature? _____

Is the room clean and neat? _____

Do I know how to operate the microphone and audiovisual equipment I will be using? _____

Do I know to whom I should speak if I need something before or during my presentation? _____

_____

Exercise: Be Prepared to Present

Complete the following exercise when you prepare for your next formal presentation.

Presentation topic _____

Reason for the presentation _____

_____

Type of event (conference, convention, workshop, and so on) and venue _____

_____

_____

Size of the audience _____

Layout of the room _____

_____

Miscellaneous details

1. When am I scheduled to speak, and how long do I have? _____

_____

_____

2. Do I need to allow time for questions? _____

3. Who else will be speaking, and what are their topics? _____

_____

_____

_____

_____

_____

_____

_____

_____

4. What kind of audiovisual equipment will I need? _____

_____

_____

_____

5. Will I need handouts or other visual aids? _____

6. Will I need a podium? _____

7. Will I need a microphone? If so, what type do I prefer? _____

_____

8. Are desks arranged in a manner conducive to my presentation? If not, what can I do about it?

_____

_____

_____

_____

9. Is the lighting sufficient? If not, how can it be improved? _____

_____

_____

_____

10. Is the room clean and neat? _____

11. What do I know about the audience? _____

_____

_____

_____

_____

_____

_____

_____

12. Is there anything the organizers need from me (bio, handouts, and so on)? _____

_____

_____

_____

_____

13. Do I know whom to contact if I have a problem? _____

_____

CHAPTER 5

Dressing for the Part

Audiences judge presenters on the whole picture, and that includes their appearance. An impeccably dressed presenter will make a positive impression and appear more credible than a disheveled one. Presenters for business should adhere to industry standards. Check the standards for the company coordinating your speaking engagement. Some industries are very conservative; others are relaxed.

If you want the audience to be accepting of you, dress the part of a professional. You will be judged on your clothing and overall appearance. Looking well-dressed and polished will boost your confidence and give you one less thing to worry about.

Leftover food or beverage stains on your tie or blouse will have the audience musing over what you had for lunch; your message will be lost. If people wonder whether you hair was caught in a storm, your message will be lost. People often associate an unkempt appearance and shoddy clothing and accessories with ineptness. Do not give your audience a reason to deliberate about an out-of-sorts appearance.

OVERALL APPEARANCE

Do not rely solely on your perception of yourself. You may believe you have an enthusiastic, outgoing persona but strike someone else as overbearing. You may feel excited but come across as uninterested. You may not be aware of your nervous gestures or tone. What you consider a chic, put-together outfit, an audience may consider too formal or too informal.

Seek opinions about your overall appearance and emotional appeal from people you trust. Consider videotaping yourself. There is nothing like seeing yourself in action in a video. Analyze your flaws and think about how best to correct them. Practice until you feel confident you are a presenter who will make an audience sit up and pay attention. Videotape yourself again to learn if you have improved.

Study presenters you admire (either in person or via videotape, webinars, or television). What is it about them that grabs your attention and holds it? Analyze their eye contact, voice, language usage, posture, gestures, and dress. How can you best emulate their presentation style? What makes you feel you can trust these presenters? How can you develop credibility for your presentations?

Awkwardness will come across in your presentation if you are not at ease and prepared. Practice will alleviate much of your stress and uneasiness. As with any practice, you want to rehearse good habits, not reinforce negative ones.

There are some obvious differences between talking to an individual versus a group or between presenting to an informal audience versus a formal one. For instance, when speaking to an individual, you only have to make eye contact with him and will not have to scan the room to meet the gaze of numerous people. In most cases, you will raise the volume of your voice when speaking to a large audience and may require a microphone. You may have to dress better for a formal event and prepare visual aids and handouts differently.

However, with a little tweaking, the basic tips and techniques for successful public speaking and presentations work for all situations.

DRESSING THE PART

Always look your best when you are presenting, whether your audience consists of a handful of people or hundreds. Your audience will have a hard time taking you seriously if you do not portray yourself as a professional. Depending on the situation, you will want to dress in a business formal or casual fashion. An informal situation might call for business casual slacks and jackets, while a formal conference may require a business suit for both men and women.

When in doubt, it is better to overdress rather than underdress. However, that does not mean party clothing. Avoid flashy styles and bright, dazzling colors and prints that might distract the audience. If you need assistance with your appearance, consult a department store employee in the clothing department. Women can also take advantage of cosmetic counter employees to obtain makeup advice or a total makeover.

In all cases, clothing should be appropriate and fit well. Tight-fitting outfits cheapen the overall look. Clothing that's too large gives a sloppy appearance. You will want to be able to move around and sit comfortably. Wearing threadbare and patched clothing is out of the question. Replace any worn or tattered clothing. The same goes for shabby shoes and accessories.

Be sure to try on new outfits during a dress rehearsal before the presentation to ensure proper fit and appropriateness.

You need not strain your budget to find good-quality clothing and accessories. Many consignment shops and outlets offer excellent buys on famous name-brand clothing and accessories.

Fabrics

Purchase the best quality clothing your budget allows. Choose top-quality, easy-to-care-for fabrics that will provide years of wear. Consider wools, linens, silks, and cottons in conservative colors, prints, and plaids.

Clothing should be impeccably clean and neatly pressed. Dry clean or wash and press after each wearing. Repair tears and replace missing buttons. If the repairs are noticeable, discard the outfit.

Shoes and Belts

Shoes should be polished and in top condition. Leather is best. Do not wear a new pair of shoes for the first time during a presentation. The shoes may feel comfortable in the store, but wearing them in a stressful situation standing in front of an audience for an extended period of time is a different story. You do not want to be preoccupied with aching feet and legs.

Belts should complement your outfit. Men should wear leather. Women's belts should match their hemline or other accessories. Belts should fit well and not be too long or too short.

Purses, Briefcases, and Computer Bags

Choose high-quality purses, briefcases, and computer bags in styles and basic colors that will go well with several different outfits. If possible, chose leather. Women should not carry both a purse and a briefcase but stuff a small wristlet into their briefcase or computer bag.

Jewelry

Keep jewelry to a minimum so as not to distract the audience. Jewelry should complement your outfit and be subtle. Remove jewelry from noticeable piercings other than women's ears.

Women should avoid dangling, noisy bracelets and necklaces. They may wear modest earrings and a necklace, a watch, a ring, and a simple bracelet. Avoid wearing rings on every finger and rows of earrings in each ear.

Men should limit jewelry to a watch and a ring.

Hair, Nails, Makeup, and Perfume

A quality cut and up-to-date hairstyle will make you feel and look good. If you have not updated your hairstyle for years, consult a hair stylist. Avoid extreme styles and colors. If you dye your hair, keep up with coloring to avoid having a different root color.

Nails should be clean and manicured. If polished, colors should be understated.

Avoid perfumes and colognes or use a light touch. People in the audience may be allergic.

Women should wear makeup that enhances their appearance. Use a light touch when applying makeup.

Dressing Tips for Women

◆ Wear a suit for presentations.

◆ Choose blues, gray, and black for suits and jackets.

◆ Choose white or pale colors for blouses.

◆ Avoid splashy prints and wild color patterns.

◆ Wear neutral colored hose with closed toe pumps.

◆ Shoe color should match hemline; shoes should be polished and well kept.

◆ Skirt hems should hit the knee or slightly below.

◆ Avoid formal party dresses.

◆ Avoid plunging necklines.

◆ Clothing should fit well, not too tight.

◆ Avoid fad fashions.

◆ Makeup should enhance features and be applied with a light touch.

◆ Choose a classic hairstyle; dyed hair should be an appropriate color.

◆ Limit jewelry to simple earrings, a necklace, a bracelet, a watch, and a ring.

Dressing Tips for Men

◆ Wear a suit for presentations.

◆ Choose blues, gray, and black for suits and jackets.

◆ Choose white or pale colors for long-sleeved shirts.

◆ Avoid patterned suits.

◆ Choose a conservative tie in a color to match the suit.

◆ Wear dress socks in a color to match the suit.

◆ Wear leather dress shoes in a color to match the suit; shoes should be polished and well kept.

◆ Wear clothing that is tailored to fit well.

◆ Choose a classic hairstyle.

◆ Trim beard and mustache neatly.

◆ Limit jewelry to a watch and a ring.

Complete the following checklist when preparing for your next presentation.

Dress for Success Checklist	Yes	No
I have chosen an outfit appropriate for my presentation.		
My clothing fits properly.		
I have chosen quality fabrics.		
My clothing and shoes are in style.		
My outfit is not flashy or too brightly colored.		
My outfit is clean and pressed.		
My shoes are polished and in good repair.		
My accessories are appropriate for the occasion.		
My accessories are clean and neat.		
My hairstyle is appropriate and up to date.		
My entire appearance is impeccable.		
I have avoided perfume and cologne.		
I have removed jewelry from unusual piercings.		
I have covered tattoos.		
I have used good hygiene.		

You should have answered yes to each item in the checklist. Work toward correcting any negative answers.

Exercise: Check Your Appearance

Fill out the following exercise the next time you prepare to give a presentation.

Topic _____

Event and venue _____

Outfit I will wear _____

_____

_____

_____

Shoes I will wear _____

My shoes are polished and free from wear _____

Accessories I will wear _____

_____

_____

I have an updated hairstyle proper for presentations _____

I have covered tattoos and removed unusual piercings _____

I have used proper hygiene habits _____

Exercise: Research Professional Attire

Find examples of professionally dressed individuals to emulate by reading magazines, newsletters, and newspapers and by researching online.

Exercise: Assess Your Wardrobe

Make a list of professional attire you currently own and another list of attire you need to obtain.

Exercise: Analyze Professionals and Their Attire

Watch videos of professional speakers on television or online, and take note of their clothing and hairstyles.

PART III

Delivering the Content

CHAPTER 6

Focusing on Your Audience

Presentations are all about the audience. To be effective, your speech must be audience-centered. Everything you say should be based on your specific audience's needs and wants. Those individuals who do not believe they need what you are offering will have a difficult time concentrating on what you say and may not listen to your message. To build a connection with your presentation participants, give them what they want and need. They must also find you a credible expert on the subject matter you are discussing.

Your first job in planning then should be to ask yourself why the audience is coming to hear you and how you can get them to trust you are providing information that will benefit them directly. The answers to those questions must be relevant to your topic and how you present it; otherwise, you will have a gap between what the audience expects to hear and what you present.

ASSESSING AUDIENCE WANTS AND NEEDS

Typically, your audience members will want to know your presentation's value for them. Usual questions that audience members may be asking themselves include these:

- ✦ What's in it for me if I listen to this presentation?
- ✦ What do I need from this presenter?
- ✦ Why should I spend my valuable time attending this presentation?
- ✦ Why should I listen to this particular speaker?
- ✦ Is this speaker credible?
- ✦ Is this speaker an expert on this topic?
- ✦ How can this speaker solve my problem (or give me knowledge or earn me money, and so on)?
- ✦ Will I learn about new opportunities available to me?
- ✦ Will I be able to solve my problems (or gain knowledge or earn money, and so on) after listening to this presentation?

Knowing what your audience needs will help you craft a presentation that targets their particular requirements and interests. Is there any way you can send a checklist or short questionnaire to participants before the event? If so, develop a simple survey and send it. If the number of attendees makes it impractical to have everyone fill out a questionnaire, consider taking a sampling of the participants. If you cannot survey the individuals who will participate in the presentation, could the organizers give you background information on them?

KNOWING YOUR AUDIENCE

Knowing your audience members' backgrounds and possible expectations will help you slant a speech toward their viewpoint and subsequently generate interest in your talk. To increase chances of a successful presentation, learn as much as possible about your audience. Find answers to questions like these:

- ✦ Who is in my audience?
- ✦ What do I know about my audience members' backgrounds and experiences?
- ✦ What does my audience know about my topic?
- ✦ Will my audience be open to what I have to say, or will they reject my message?
- ✦ How will my audience benefit from what I have to say (for example, solve problems, make money, gain knowledge, and so on)?
- ✦ What does my audience expect to receive from me?
- ✦ What does my audience think I should provide them or tell them?
- ✦ What does my audience need from me?
- ✦ Do I need anything from my audience?
- ✦ How can I involve my audience in the presentation?

✦ How will I appeal to the different learning styles of my audience?

✦ What examples and visuals can I use that pertain to this specific audience?

✦ Will my audience readily understand the meaning of my words?

✦ What objections might my audience have about what I say?

✦ What is the knowledge level of my audience?

✦ What are the demographics for my audience (sex, age, race, culture, and so on)?

✦ Does my audience expect hands-on participation?

✦ Is there anything I need to know about my audience's interests and lifestyles?

✦ What format would best suit this audience?

Answers to these questions will let you see things from the audience's perspective and help you prepare a message specific to that particular group.

To develop an audience survey, select questions from the preceding list and add others you may want answered. Limit the number of questions, or participants will be discouraged from completing the survey. Arrange the questions in a pleasing, easy-to-follow format, add directions for completing the survey, and send it to participants. The survey could be included in publicity materials or be mailed or emailed separately.

When it is not feasible to survey participants ahead of time, you could ask questions at the start of the presentation by requesting a show of hands in answer.

Complete the following checklist.

Know the Audience Checklist	Yes	No
I know something of my audience's background.		
I know something of my audience's demographics.		
I know my audience's knowledge level of my topic.		
I have defined the benefits my audience will gain by listening to my presentation.		
I know what I need my audience to do (say, think, learn) following my presentation.		
I have identified possible objectives my audience may raise.		
I have developed ways for my audience to participate in my presentation.		
I have developed visuals for this specific audience and presentation.		
I have considered my audience's various learning styles.		
I will use language my audience can understand.		
I have chosen a format suited to this audience.		

You should have answered yes to each item in the checklist. Work toward correcting any negative answers.

MEETING YOUR AUDIENCE'S NEEDS

Once you have a snapshot of your audience, you will be able to address their needs, wants, and concerns through the message you deliver to them. Prepare your talk based on the information you gathered about them. Structure your presentation and create slides, handouts, and other visuals that appeal to them.

Let the audience know why you are the best person to give the presentation. Back up your credentials with solid information they can use. Explain the benefit of listening to your talk and taking the action you desire from them.

If your audience knows something about your subject, use that to your advantage by building on their knowledge and soliciting their opinions during discussion periods. If the audience knows little to nothing of the subject matter, start with the basics when addressing them. Language and audiovisual aids should be at a level they understand.

If you feel your audience will not be receptive to your message, try to find some common ground from which to work. For instance, if you are given the task of helping laid off employees secure new jobs, they may resent you as much as the company that fired them. Be sympathetic to their plight, and never act superior because you have a job. Begin by letting them know you are there to prepare and assist them in finding another comparable job. Start right in with the benefits of taking your advice and then detail the assistance you can offer. If you have been laid off in the past, share that story and the happy ending of your present job to build camaraderie.

ENGAGING YOUR AUDIENCE

How can you influence or inform people if you cannot hold their attention? Keeping audiences engaged is a central goal of presenters. How do you hold people's attention and encourage them to participate? To gain the audience's attention and hold it throughout the presentation, you must provide information they want and need to hear in an interesting, lively manner with as much enthusiasm as you can deliver. Once you have the relevant, appealing information gathered and written in an attention-grabbing format, work on presenting it in an exciting, inspiring way. Chapter 7, "Perfecting Your Delivery Method and Pacing," provides tips for energizing your presentation.

Another way to engage your audience is to let them know you are open to questions and welcome them at any point in your presentation. Tell them it is fine to interrupt you. However, if you are worried about time constraints or you feel it is best if your audience waits until the end of your presentation to ask questions, let them know you have planned a question-and-answer period following the presentation. Ask people to write down their questions and ask them at that time.

If your audience does not ask questions or does not participate in any way, you can question them. Request a show of hands for specific questions, ask ones that make the audience think about your subject, or ask ones that help to clarify what they want. All of your questions must be relevant to your talk and overall topic; otherwise, your presentation may spin in a direction you do not want it to take.

You might ask for a show of hands regarding the following kinds of questions:

✦ How many of you attended a similar presentation?

✦ How many of you are familiar with this subject?

✦ How many of you have experienced a similar situation (or problem) at work?

✦ How many of you have used this product (or service, information, software, and so on)?

✦ How many of you have studied this subject before?

✦ How many of you have ever come across the need for this information?

✦ Who here can use help solving a similar problem (or need more information or can use more money, and so on)?

Sometimes you want to get your audience actively involved and generate a robust discussion. To stimulate a discussion, consider asking questions such as these:

✦ What are you hoping to learn today?

✦ What are your particular needs with regard to this topic?

✦ What do you think will happen if you try these techniques in your workplace?

✦ How do you handle these kinds of problems?

✦ What would you do in a similar situation?

✦ What is an example of how you handled this type of problem (or raised money or gained knowledge, and so on)?

✦ How have you used this product (or service, information, software, and so on)?

✦ How can this information help you solve your particular problems (or earn you money or increase your knowledge, and so on)?

✦ What is an example of a problem related to this topic that you have encountered?

✦ What would convince you to try this solution (or knowledge or product, and so on)?

Another way to encourage involvement is to have the audience participate in activities or demonstrations. You can use icebreakers, games, group activities, handout exercises, hands-on experiments, and the like.

Involving your audience gives you the opportunity to learn something of what they want or need and lets you know they are attentive. You might also be able to determine if you are getting your message across or if you need to clarify points. In addition, audience participation may alleviate audience boredom.

Complete the following checklist when preparing for your next presentation.

Engaging the Audience	Yes	No
I have an open and engaging persona.		
I will tell stories or use ice breakers to build rapport with the audience.		
I have prepared an informative talk.		
I will attempt to learn what my audience expects from my presentation.		
I will learn something about my audience and their needs.		
I will demonstrate how my presentation will benefit the audience.		

Engaging the Audience	Yes	No
I have prepared handouts and visuals to enhance my presentation.		
I have prepared questions to ask the audience and encourage their participation.		
I have prepared activities and demonstrations to encourage audience participation.		
I will welcome questions from the audience.		

You should have answered yes to each item in the checklist. Work toward correcting any negative answers.

SHOWING INTEREST IN YOUR AUDIENCE

If you want the audience to be receptive to you and your message, express a sincere interest in them. Build rapport through examples and stories that let them know you understand their concerns and you can relate to them.

Provide time for questions. Take questions as they are asked if it is within your timeframe and structure, or defer them until the question-and-answer session at the end of your talk. Respect the audience's knowledge of the subject matter and their opinions when answering questions or engaging them in discussions. Avoid displaying a superior, condescending attitude even if an audience member makes an incorrect assumption or is opinionated. Gently steer the individual to the correct answer. Center your answers on your audience's concerns.

Talking down to your audience, preaching, criticizing, or making sarcastic remarks will alienate and upset them. Negative emotions will destroy rapport and the opportunity to influence individuals to behave or react as you would want. In addition, avoid acting like a know-it-all or braggart or stretching the truth. Keep all destructive, undesirable comments and annoying mannerisms out of your presentation.

Your audience members may have different learning styles. For instance, some may prefer to see visuals to get the message; others may prefer listening to a speaker; some may want to perform a hands-on demonstration. The best presentations incorporate various methods of delivery—visual aids, lecture, time for note taking, demonstrations, and exercises to complete—to appeal to all of these listeners.

Make eye contact with as many audience members as you can, but do not let your eyes roam around the room at random. Smile and encourage audience participation.

Exercise: Relate to Your Audience

Plan your next presentation by completing the following:

Topic _____

What do you know about your audience's background? _____

_____

_____

_____

_____

_____

_____

Does your audience know anything about your topic? _____

Have you used language your audience can relate to and understand? _____

Have you prepared ways to build rapport with your audience? _____

Will your audience be receptive to the information you present? _____

Have you approached your topic in a way that your talk is composed for this particular audience?

_____

Have you outlined the benefits of listening to your presentation? _____

How will you engage your audience? _____

_____

_____

_____

_____

_____

_____

List the main points you want your audience to remember about your presentation.

_____

_____

_____

_____

_____

_____

What visual aids are best suited to this audience? _____

_____

_____

_____

_____

_____

_____

_____

Have you allowed time for questions from the audience? _____

What handouts are best suited to this audience? _____

_____

_____

_____

_____

_____

_____

What questions can you ask to get your audience involved? _____

_____

_____

_____

_____

_____

_____

_____

Exercise: Survey Your Audience

When you plan your next presentation, create a survey to learn about the audience. Choose a few questions that will give you the best indication of what you should cover in your talk. Arrange the questions in a suitable format, give detailed instructions for completing the survey, and send it to participants. You can prepare a hard copy of the questionnaire or an electronic one.

Exercise: Build Rapport with Your Audience

List three ways you can build rapport with your next audience.

_____

_____

_____

CHAPTER 7

Perfecting Your Delivery Method and Pacing

Your audience's perception of you and your message will have a bearing on whether they listen to you and accept what you have to say. Their perception may be inaccurate, but it will not matter because in their minds it is reality. Therefore, make your message and yourself appealing to that specific audience.

Create the right message exclusively for your audience. Take care with your appearance, behavior, and mannerisms. Deliver an enthusiastic, passionate, sincere talk. The compilation of these factors will create your audience's perception of you and your presentation. Do your best to make a positive impact.

CREDIBILITY

Your credibility is critical to the success of your presentation. No matter how carefully you craft your speech or prepare your supplemental materials, the audience will not react favorably or take the action you desire unless they believe you.

To begin with, *you* must believe in what you are saying and doing to convey that essence to others. Your visual presence, voice, words, and supporting materials must lead your audience to believe you are honest and trustworthy. If the audience thinks you are dishonest, they will have a difficult time receiving your message, let alone acting on it. Everything you say will be subject to scrutiny and acceptance or dismissal. You must connect with each listener on an emotional level—you must be believed.

An effective presentation informs or persuades an audience by producing credible facts in a visually appealing way. For instance, making eye contact with the audience, speaking in a sincere tone, and portraying confidence will encourage your audience to believe your words and visual aids. On the other hand, faulty information, weak visual performance, and poor preparation will sabotage your presentation and ultimately your message.

When your audience thinks you are credible, you may have an easier time influencing them to accept the premise of your message and the facts as you present them.

Inconsistency in your presentation will have your audience questioning your credibility and asking themselves why they are listening to you. You may have important, factual information, but if the audience questions your delivery, the message may be lost. You may have a great visual presence, but if your information is unbelievable, your message may be lost. Therefore, it is important to work on the total presentation to gain your audience's trust.

Complete the following checklist.

Credibility Checklist	Yes	No
Do you consistently present credible information?		
Do you believe the information you are presenting?		
Have you verified your information sources?		
Have you sufficient facts to support your key points?		
Does your voice sound convincing?		
Do you exhibit a credible visual presence?		
Are you doing all you can to promote your credibility?		
Do you feel your audience believes you?		

You should have answered yes to each item in the checklist. Work toward correcting any negative answers.

FACIAL EXPRESSIONS

Smiling is one of the best ways to make a connection with others and build rapport. A radiant smile dominates the face. Be generous with your smile, and make it sincere and welcoming. People will be more receptive to your message if they perceive you as friendly and likeable.

People can tell when a smile is forced. If anxiety about speaking in front of groups undermines your smile, practice your presentation over and over until you feel comfortable maintaining a smile.

Negative facial expressions, including frowns, sneers, smirks, forehead creases, lip biting, clenched jaws, pursed lips, stiff faces, and the like will drive a wedge between you and the audience. A stone-faced presenter will have a difficult time holding an audience's attention and convincing them to act or react the way he intends. Be conscious of these and other nervous ticks and negative facial expressions; practice eliminating them.

Do not cover your mouth as you speak, as it may convey that you are not being truthful or are nervous.

Complete the following checklist.

Facial Expression Checklist	Yes	No
Do you exhibit a sincere welcoming smile?		
Is your face relaxed?		
Is your jaw relaxed?		
Is your face animated when speaking with people?		
Do you take care not to frown or bite your lip?		
Do you take care not to smirk?		

You should have answered yes to each item in the checklist. Work toward correcting any negative answers.

VOICE

Is your voice monotone, flat, garbled, screechy, halting, or inarticulate? Do you mumble or stutter? Do you ramble or race through your speech so fast that your audience misses most of it? If any of these poor habits describes you, the audience may tune you out or be so focused on the annoying habit that they miss your message.

Make your tone appealing by varying your inflection as you emphasize key words and phrases. Speak naturally and clearly. Pronounce words correctly and distinctly.

Stressed speakers and those who worry about forgetting their speech tend to race through their talks or speak in a halting manner. Remind yourself to speak at a normal speed the audience members can follow. Your audience may be unfamiliar with the material and need to digest what you say. Even if they are familiar, some information may be new to them. Speak at a moderate rate and pause occasionally. Pay attention to your audience's nonverbal signs to determine if they are grasping your message.

You may want to have a colleague keep track of the time while you speak and signal you at intervals so you know if you are pacing yourself properly. If you find you are running out of time, finish the speech with the critical information and forget the rest. Another option is to make your summary succinct.

Avoid both shouting and speaking too softly. People sensitive to noise will be irritated by loud voices, and people who must strain to hear you may tune you out or become annoyed because they continue to miss information. A person who misses something you said may disturb the person next to him to ask what was said. Now two people are at risk of losing additional information. If several people ask you to repeat information, you may need to adjust your volume or the microphone.

Using microphones can pose pitfalls. If the microphone is mounted on a lectern, you must speak directly into it. If you turn away from the microphone to look at a slide screen or elsewhere, you risk not being heard. A lapel-mounted mic allows you to move around the room, but take care not to loosen the mic or say something you do not want your audience to overhear.

Knowing your material and practicing ahead of time will help you eliminate "ah," and "um," or similar habits from your speech.

Complete the following checklist.

Voice Checklist	Yes	No
Is your tone interesting and enthusiastic?		
Do you speak at a normal rate?		
Is your tone sincere and credible?		
Do you speak clearly and distinctly?		
Is your voice audible?		
Have you checked the pronunciation of unfamiliar words in your presentation?		
Are you mindful of any poor speech habits you have?		
Have you practiced your presentation?		
Have you practiced your presentation using a microphone if you are unfamiliar speaking with one?		

You should have answered yes to each item in the checklist. Work toward correcting any negative answers.

EYE CONTACT

Your eyes can convey excitement, enthusiasm, and confidence as well as boredom, indifference, and nervousness. You can intimidate a person or make him or her feel relaxed. You can show you are involved in the conversation or detached. Make the most of eye contact with your audience by practicing positive techniques.

Where do you look when presenting to an audience? Ideally, you will want to make eye contact with your audience, but avoid staring in one spot or at one section for too long. Choose an audience member or section of the room and maintain eye contact for five to ten seconds before moving on to someone else. If your audience is large, the people around the person you glance at will get the feeling you are looking at them, too.

Avoid closing your eyes for several seconds while you think about what you want to say. You may give the appearance that you have forgotten what to say or need a few moments; your audience could then feel disconnected from you. Excessive blinking or squinting may make people nervous or uncomfortable; control your blinking, and do not squint.

Try to make eye contact with as many people in the audience as possible to show you are interested in communicating with the entire group. Scan the room occasionally to determine how your message is being received, but do not give the impression your eyes are darting from one person to another or all around the room. Assess your audience. Do people appear to understand your message, or are they confused? Do people look bored, or are they nodding off? By gauging your audience's reactions, you can adjust your presentation as needed.

In some cultures it is rude to stare or make prolonged eye contact, so be mindful of cultural customs. If you are speaking internationally, learn what is acceptable in that culture.

Do not turn your back on your audience to operate audiovisual equipment or to read from slides. Glancing at note cards or slides is fine, but do not read from your notes, handouts, or slides. If you read your presentation to the audience, many will wonder why they bothered to attend in person when you could have handed them a copy of your notes. An audience comes to a presentation to hear a speaker, not to listen to a reader. Effective presentations are led by speakers who are not bound to their notes, slides, or handouts.

If you are giving a television interview, look at the person you are speaking to; do not look directly at the camera.

Complete the following checklist.

Eye Contact Checklist	Yes	No
Do you make eye contact with your audience?		
Do you scan the audience checking to see how your message is received?		
Do you keep eye contact for 5–10 seconds and avoid staring?		
Do you avoid turning your head in too many directions while looking at your audience?		
Do you avoid turning your back on the audience?		
Do you avoid reading from your notes or from your slides?		
Do you avoid excessive blinking and squinting?		
Do you avoid glancing away from your audience out of nervousness?		
Are you mindful of cultural differences with regard to eye contact?		

You should have answered yes to each item in the checklist. Work toward correcting any negative answers.

Exercise: Assess Your Eye Contact with Others

The next time you engage in a conversation with an individual, pay particular attention to where you look. Ask yourself:

- ✦ Do you maintain eye contact?
- ✦ Do you glance around at other parts of the person's face or hair or shoulders?
- ✦ Do you glance around the room or other surroundings?
- ✦ Do you stare?
- ✦ Do you blink excessively or squint?

Pay attention to where you look the next time you engage in a conversation with a large group. Ask yourself:

- ✦ Do you maintain eye contact?
- ✦ Do you glance at different individuals in the group?
- ✦ Do you glance around the room or other surroundings?
- ✦ Do you stare at any one individual?
- ✦ Do you blink excessively or squint?

Exercise: Assess a Speaker's Eye Contact with You

The next time you engage in a conversation with an individual, pay particular attention to where he or she looks. Ask yourself:

- ✦ Does the speaker maintain eye contact with you?
- ✦ Does the speaker glance around at other parts of your face or hair or shoulders?
- ✦ Does the speaker glance around the room or other surroundings?
- ✦ Does the speaker stare at you?
- ✦ Does the speaker blink excessively or squint?

Pay close attention to the speaker the next time you attend a presentation where you are part of a large group or audience. Ask yourself:

- ✦ Does the speaker maintain eye contact with several people in the group or audience?
- ✦ Does the speaker seem to be spinning in all directions trying to take in too many faces at once?
- ✦ Does the speaker glance around the room or other surroundings?
- ✦ Does the speaker stare at any one person or section of the group too long?
- ✦ Does the speaker blink excessively or squint?

POSTURE

Stand tall and poised if you want to be perceived as a confident professional. An erect posture commands respect and signals that you are self-assured. However, do not exaggerate to the point of giving the impression you are arrogant or snobbish.

Balance your weight so you do not appear to lean back on one hip or slouch. Keep your shoulders back. When you slump or stoop your shoulders, you give the impression you are awkward, shy, insecure, or apprehensive.

Watch out for nervous movements such as constant shifting from one foot to the other, tapping feet, crossing and uncrossing legs over, pacing or walking too briskly through an audience, leaning on walls or a podium, and similar motions. Videotape yourself to get a good picture of how you carry yourself when talking and interacting with others.

Avoid being bound to a desk or podium during your presentation. Stand while speaking to give weight to your words. Step away from the podium occasionally and walk around the room. If you must sit, mind your posture and sit erect.

Your arms and hands should appear relaxed at your side unless you are gesturing or making a point. Avoid awkward, uncomfortable positions such as a permanent bend at the elbows or clenched fists that detract from your appearance.

When sitting, maintain an erect posture; avoid slouching in your seat. Cross your feet at the ankles or keep them flat on the floor.

Complete the following checklist.

Posture Checklist	Yes	No
Do you stand and walk straight?		
Do you keep your shoulders back?		
Do you hold your head erect?		
Do you have a balanced stance?		
Are your hands and arms relaxed?		
Are your legs relaxed?		
Do you walk with confidence?		
Do you walk at a normal pace?		
Do you sit up straight?		

You should have answered yes to each item in the checklist. Work toward correcting any negative answers.

GESTURES

Mannerisms can either make or break a presentation. Some animation will liven up your presentation, but overusing gestures can be annoying. Find a balance that is natural and comfortable for you.

Keep your arms and hands relaxed at your side whenever you do not need to gesture to make a point. Too much gesturing may give the impression you are over-exaggerating. Awkward gestures will make you look uncomfortable and clumsy. Annoying gestures include fingering necklaces and earrings, pulling at ties, playing with hair, tugging at clothing, biting the lip, clicking the tongue or fingers, and the like.

Find out how you look to others by asking a trusted friend or associate to analyze your gestures, or video-tape yourself. Concentrate on identifying and eliminating nervous and annoying gestures. Choose the worst habit you have and work on removing it. Then systematically work on another habit and another. Trying to eliminate all negative gestures at the same time may discourage you, as it is difficult to break bad habits.

Complete the following checklist.

Positive Gestures Checklist	Exhibit	Hope to Improve	Do Not Exhibit
Smiling			
Nodding			
Waving			
Laughing			
Making eye contact			
Relaxing arms and legs			
Relaxing jaw and face			
Standing straight			
Keeping shoulders back			
Keeping head erect			
Maintaining confident, balanced stance			
Using hand motions appropriately			
Shaking hands properly			

You should have answered yes to exhibiting each gesture in the checklist. Work toward correcting any gestures you hope to improve or do not exhibit.

Complete the checklist on the following page.

Negative Gestures Checklist	Exhibit	Hope to Improve	Do Not Exhibit
Pulling at clothing			
Blinking excessively			
Pursing lips; frowning			
Tapping fingers or feet			
Toying with hair, jewelry, and so on			
Darting eyes			
Avoiding eye contact			
Clicking tongue or fingers			
Slouching			
Flailing arms and hands			
Trembling hands			
Sweating hands			
Clenching fist			
Clenching teeth/jaw			
Frowning			
Tapping feet			
Shifting from one foot to the other			
Pacing			
Displaying nervous ticks			
Mumbling			
Covering mouth			
Fidgeting			
Biting lip			
Smirking			
Raising eyebrows			
Slouching shoulders			
Putting hands on hips			

You should not exhibit the gestures in the previous checklist. Work toward correcting any negative behaviors.

Exercise: Analyze a Speaker

Watch a political speech, and critique the politician's facial expressions, eye contact, voice, and gestures. Watch a television news interviewer who is covering a scene where he has to move around, and critique his posture. Practice emulating these individuals if their posture and gestures are positive.

Exercise: Analyze Your Presentation

Ask a trusted friend or associate to analyze your gestures during your next presentation.

PERSONAL ATTRIBUTES

Positive personal attributes, including mannerisms and character traits, can be used to engage and to persuade your audience. Character traits such as credibility, honesty, friendliness, efficiency, enthusiasm, and the like will help you build rapport with an audience and gain their trust. Negative character traits will have the opposite effect.

Be generous in your desire to help others succeed by being the best presenter you can be. Realize your capacity to change the lives of your audience for the better by bringing them information on your subject.

Show your enthusiasm and passion. Getting excited and believing in what you say will encourage the audience to get excited and to trust you.

Avoid negative traits and their accompanying gestures as discussed earlier.

Exercise: Assess Your Character Traits

Check the appropriate boxes to indicate whether you exhibit the positive character traits, hope to improve in that area, or do not exhibit the trait. Ideally, you should exhibit all of the traits or aspire to achieve them. Add other positive traits you feel would benefit you as a presenter.

Character Traits Checklist	Exhibit	Hope to Improve	Do Not Exhibit
Honest			
Credible			
Sincere			
Friendly			
Helpful			
Calm			
Confident			
Efficient			
Dependable			

Character Traits Checklist	Exhibit	Hope to Improve	Do Not Exhibit
Discreet			
Knowledgeable			
Courteous			
Organized			
Good Listener			
Supportive			
Motivated			

You should have answered yes to exhibiting each character trait in the checklist. Work toward correcting any traits you hope to improve or do not exhibit.

QUESTIONS

Welcome questions throughout your presentation. It shows your audience is attentive and interested in the topic. Offer a brief response based on their knowledge. On the other hand, do not get sidetracked by questions or the person asking them. If numerous interruptions become a distraction for you or for the audience, ask people to hold their questions until the question-and-answer period at the end of your presentation.

HUMOR

Using humor is appropriate in your presentation, but you do not want to fall off the stage laughing. A short humorous story can build rapport with your audience, but avoid inappropriate humor and humor at someone else's expense. Skip the jokes and opt for a general comment about life, yourself, or your subject that will bring a smile or laughter.

GAMES AND ACTIVITIES

Involve your audience in games or activities that will help them assimilate your message. If a demonstration will help the audience members understand how something works, arrange one. If you want people to get to know each other better, have them do an ice-breaking activity or two. Plan activities that will make their learning easier. Keep the activities and participants moving along so as not to exceed your time limit.

Note-taking and completing exercises on handouts help attendees gather information, practice what they are learning, and integrate information.

Exercise: Analyze a Presentation

The next time you attend a presentation, analyze how the speaker uses humor to build rapport with the audience. Think of similar ways that you can build rapport with your future audiences through humor.

CHAPTER 8

Practicing Your Presentation

After spending hours researching your topic and preparing a wonderful speech complete with pleasing visual aids, you will not want to sabotage your presentation by failing to rehearse before you present in front of others. Practicing the delivery of your speech can build your confidence, improve your performance, aid pacing and timing, and relieve some of your anxiety about standing in front of people and speaking. Practicing over and over and including a dress rehearsal will help you deliver a skillful presentation.

PRACTICE

Put in sufficient, thoughtful time to practice your remarks. No matter how confident you feel, skipping or rushing through the practice step could ruin your talk. Practice with your visuals to ensure they are appropriate for your speech and you have sufficient time to incorporate them. If you will be presenting at a large, formal event, you may want to run through a complete dress rehearsal. This will give you a sense of the practicality and comfort of your attire. For instance, can you stand, sit, and move about freely? Are your shoes comfortable?

Whenever you practice, do not silently read over the speech. Talk aloud so you hear the rhythm of the words and sentences. Reading your talk may not take as long as speaking it, especially if you intend to use visual aids. Go through the presentation from beginning to end, and time it to determine if you are adhering to your time limit. By practicing in the manner you will be presenting, you will become aware of whether you need to adjust your pacing. It is better to find out in the practice run if your speech will go on too long or come up short, rather than the during the actual presentation.

Rehearsing the entire presentation will allow you to uncover spots where you are nervous or uncomfortable or those times when you lose track of your thoughts. You will be able to determine if your words and visuals coordinate.

Videotape your rehearsal if possible. The video will show you where you need to improve and what you are doing right. For instance, you may feel you are portraying an enthusiastic, energetic persona, but the video may contradict that idea. You may not realize you have nervous habits until the video displays them for you.

VOLUNTEER

Another way to practice and improve your presentation skill is to seek out opportunities to speak. These opportunities are great for honing speaking and performance skills. If you are a beginner, you might volunteer to give small, informal presentations in your workplace or for organizations to which you belong. Let people know you are available and what your areas of expertise are.

After developing confidence speaking to small groups and increasing your expertise with each presentation, you may want to broaden your appearances to include formal events such as conferences and conventions.

ENLIST HELP

If possible, persuade a colleague or friend to listen to your practice presentation and evaluate your efforts. Choose someone you trust to be honest. You will want answers to the following questions:

+ Are my content and delivery credible?
+ Is my content appropriate for my audience?
+ Did I deliver the content in an interesting way?
+ Did I deliver the content in a logical, organized manner?
+ Were my key points clear?
+ Did I offer sufficient supporting information?

- ✦ Did I hold your interest throughout?
- ✦ Did I use positive gestures, such as maintaining appropriate eye contact, smiling, displaying confidence, exhibiting erect posture, and the like?
- ✦ Did I display negative nervous habits? If so, what were they?
- ✦ Did I appear relaxed and calm?
- ✦ Was my voice clear, energetic, and free of nervous ticks?
- ✦ Did I have a professional appearance? If not, how can I improve?
- ✦ Did I appear passionate?
- ✦ Did I make good use of visual aids?
- ✦ Were my visual aids appropriate?
- ✦ Where do you feel I need to improve?
- ✦ What general comments do you have for me?

Complete the following checklist.

Practice Checklist	Yes	No
I have practiced my presentation from beginning to end until I am comfortable delivering it.		
I have practiced aloud.		
I rehearsed in the outfit I will wear for the presentation.		
I have used my visual aids while practicing.		
I have practiced with the equipment I will be using during the presentation.		
I know my material well.		
I videotaped my practice presentation.		
I assessed the videotape of my practice presentation.		
I have enlisted a friend to listen to and evaluate my presentation.		
I have received informative feedback from my friend.		
I have sought ways to improve my presentation.		

You should have answered yes to each item in the checklist. Work toward correcting any negative answers.

Exercise: Practice Your Presentation

Practice your presentation. Ask a friend or two to be your audience. After the presentation, ask the friends for feedback regarding your content, gestures, delivery manner, appearance, credibility, and the like.

Exercise: Videotape Your Presentation

Videotape your practice presentation. Dress in the outfit you will wear for the presentation. Watch the video and assess your content, gestures, delivery manner, appearance, credibility, and the like.

KNOW YOUR MATERIAL

Know your material so well that if you had to, you could deliver your presentation without notes or visual aids; however, do not memorize the speech to the point you sound rehearsed and monotone. Visuals and note cards should only be consulted to nudge your memory.

Commit key points to memory. Strive to drive your key points home by repeating them several times throughout the presentation. Use phrases to signal the importance of key points: "It is important…" "Critical to this message is…" "The main thing to remember…" The biggest takeaway from this presentation is…."

Support your speech with personal examples of your experience with the topic. Doing so will demonstrate you are an expert in that area. You may be asked tough questions regarding your presentation. Becoming an expert on the material will help you answer questions effectively.

Show your enthusiasm. If you are not passionate about your topic and subject matter, you will have a difficult time convincing your audience and gaining their trust. Why should the audience care about what you say if you give the appearance you do not?

DIMINISH ANXIETY AND STRESS

Anxiety and stress cause a variety of physical and mental conditions including sweating; trembling hands and legs; fiddling with jewelry, ties, pens, or visual aids; stuttering or shaky voice; heart tremors, dry mouth, nausea, difficulty concentrating, forgetfulness, racing or pounding heart, tense muscles, and so on.

Knowing your material well and practicing the presentation several times will build your confidence and help diminish anxiety and stress.

Some stress is due to worrying about making a mistake. Do not let mistakes intimidate you. Everyone makes a mistake at some point. Tell yourself you will keep calm and continue with your speech if you happen to make a mistake. Audience members may not notice a slight mistake (for example, if you skip over a minor note). If you make a glaring error, you might try pointing it out with a bit of humor and then giving the correct information.

RELIEVE STRESS

One of the best ways to alleviate stress regarding your presentation is to be well prepared. Plan, organize, and practice the presentation. As you become confident that your presentation is first-rate, stress will diminish. The more often you speak in front of others, the more comfortable you may become.

Believe in your content and its value to the audience. Trust the audience wants to hear what you have to say.

Take steps to relieve stress before presentations by exercising some of the tips that follow.

Tips to Calm Stress

- Be prepared; know your material.
- Jot brief comments on note cards.
- Review your notes immediately before the presentation.
- Practice your presentation several times.
- Act confidently.
- Do deep breathing exercises.
- Stand and walk erect.
- Take a walk before the presentation.
- Think pleasant thoughts.
- Visualize a successful presentation.
- Familiarize yourself with the room and equipment you will be using.
- Look over your notes immediately before the presentation.
- Arrive early.
- Avoid excessive caffeine.
- Have water available throughout your talk, and take an occasional drink.
- Trust you have information the audience wants or needs.
- Discuss your nervousness with a trusted friend.

Exercise: Assess a Presentation You Attended

Think about a presentation you recently attended and answer the following questions:

1. Did you feel the information presented was credible? Why or why not?

_____

_____

_____

_____

_____

2. Was the speaker credible? If not, why?

_____

_____

_____

_____

3. Did you feel a connection to the speaker? _____

4. Was the information presented in a logical manner? _____

5. Did you understand what the presenter was trying to convey? If not, why do you think you did not understand him or her? _____

_____

_____

_____

_____

_____

6. What major points of the presentation do you remember?

_____

_____

_____

_____

_____

_____

7. Could the presentation have been improved? How?

_____

_____

_____

_____

_____

8. Did the presenter use visual aids? If so, were they effective? Why or why not? If no visual aids were used, do you feel they should have been?

_____

_____

_____

_____

_____

9. Do you feel the speaker focused on the subject matter you thought you were coming to hear about? If not, why not?

   _____

   _____

   _____

   _____

10. Did the speaker recap the main points at the end of the presentation? _____

11. Was the speaker dressed professionally? If not, did that distract you during the presentation? In what way were you distracted? _____

    _____

    _____

    _____

    _____

12. Did the speaker appear confident? _____

13. Was the speaker interesting and enthusiastic? _____

14. Did the speaker use positive or negative gestures? Were they distracting? _____

    _____

15. What overall effect did the speaker have on you? _____

    _____

    _____

    _____

    _____

16. Following the presentation, did you do as the speaker asked or react the way the speaker intended? Why or why not?

    _____

    _____

    _____

    _____

17. Did you receive a takeaway from the presentation, such as a handout, brochure, sample, or the like? If not, would you have preferred one? _____

    _____

Exercise: Describe Your Idea of an Ideal Presentation

Complete the exercise.

Describe your ideal presentation from the standpoint of a listener.

_____

_____

_____

_____

_____

_____

_____

_____

_____

How can you structure your next presentation to appeal to the listener described in the previous question?

_____

_____

_____

_____

_____

_____

_____

_____

_____

_____

_____

_____

Describe your ideal presentation with you as the speaker.

_____

_____

_____

_____

_____

_____

_____

What can you do to create your ideal presentation?

_____

_____

_____

_____

_____

_____

_____

_____

_____

_____

_____

_____

_____

CHAPTER 9

Delivering the Speech and the Wrap-Up

When the day arrives and it is time to pull everything together that you have learned, step before your audience and give a first-class presentation. Be confident, enthusiastic, professional, and entertaining. Let your audience know you are an expert on your topic and feel comfortable speaking about it. Tell them how they will benefit greatly from hearing your talk. Show the audience you are a professional from your words, your delivery of them, your efficiency, and your appearance.

USE YOUR KNOWLEDGE

If you completed the checklists and exercises throughout this book and followed the tips and techniques presented, you will have the tools to prepare for your next presentation. If you put what you learned into practice, you will have done the following:

◆ Learned all you can about your topic, the audience, and the venue.

◆ Written out your talk and made your note cards.

◆ Created appropriate handouts and other visual aids.

◆ Rehearsed your presentation in front of a friend or videotaped it if possible.

◆ Checked out the audiovisual equipment and the microphone.

◆ Made copies of handouts and any materials you plan to distribute.

◆ Made sure everything is set on the venue end.

◆ Decided what to wear, and made sure everything is cleaned and pressed.

◆ Have styled your hair and manicured your nails.

◆ Groomed yourself.

◆ Checked last-minute details, the delivery time, and your mode of transportation to the event.

Take everything you have learned from the previous chapters and plan and prepare your next presentation. Practice your speech using your visual aids until you feel comfortable. Run through a dress rehearsal the night before.

DELIVER A WINNING SPEECH

You have learned that the delivery of your speech is as important as your content. A poor presentation will turn the audience off to your words; an excellent presentation will leave them satisfied and inclined to act or react the way you intended. By following the suggestions and information presented in this book, you increase your chances of delivering a winning presentation.

The tips that follow were detailed throughout this book. Review them carefully, and employ them during your next presentation.

Tips for Giving Presentations

- Simplify complex information by using metaphors, examples, and stories.
- Support key points with first-hand experience and stories.
- Stick to your key points.
- Repeat key points throughout the presentation.
- Relate everything to your main topic.
- Show your commitment to your subject.
- State the benefit to the audience of listening to the presentation.

- Open with an attention getter.
- Ask questions and give audience members time to think about their answers.
- Make the talk relevant to the audience.
- Be honest.
- Reference credible sources and double-check them.
- Build rapport; show you care.
- Use eye contact.
- Avoid slang and jargon.
- Speak slowly and clearly.
- Vary your tone.
- Speak at an appropriate volume.
- Never talk down to your audience.
- Avoid words that stall a talk, such as ah, um, etc.
- Show your confidence.
- Be enthusiastic.
- Use appropriate humor.
- Engage the audience in games and activities.
- Finish on time.
- Prepare applicable handouts and visual aids.
- Do not overload slides with text, animations, sound, etc.
- Dress professionally.
- Wear a stylish hairstyle.
- Use proper hygiene.
- Check audiovisual equipment beforehand.
- Give ample examples.
- Research thoroughly.
- Be prepared for questions.
- Be prepared for differences of opinions.
- Anticipate what the audience wants to know.
- Do not read word for word from notes.
- Be mindful of gestures and body language.
- Avoid giving a long, boring lecture.
- Conclude with something that the audience will remember long after they leave.
- Keep your outcome in mind throughout the talk.
- Do not be bound to the podium (or desk).
- Use up-to-date information.
- Practice your presentation.

Unfortunately, even a minor slip can derail your speech. In addition to knowing what you should do, keep in mind what you should not do. Review the list below of things to avoid when giving a presentation as they will sabotage your efforts:

Things to Avoid

- Having no clear purpose
- Speaking too fast/slow/monotone
- Reading from notes
- Relying too heavily on slides
- Presenting on faulty audio visual equipment or microphone
- Not knowing how to operate the audio visual equipment or microphone you will be using during the presentation
- Using unessential and excessive slides
- Using poor-quality slides
- Acting indifferent/expressing lack of passion
- Starting or ending late
- Not making eye contact
- Overloading the audience with information
- Presenting irrelevant information
- Being unfamiliar with the information you are presenting
- Thinking you can present without practicing beforehand
- Using outdated, unreliable information

Although it seems there is much to learn and to do when it comes to giving great presentations, the process will become more familiar and easier to complete with practice. The best thing to do is to get out and speak.

Complete the following checklist.

Delivery of Presentation Checklist	Yes	No
I have prepared well for my presentation.		
I have practiced my presentation several times.		
I have made notes to use during my presentation.		
I have created audio visuals.		
I have made copies of needed handouts.		

Delivery of Presentation Checklist	Yes	No
I have checked equipment and last-minute details.		
I am well groomed and professionally dressed.		
I intend to project a confident, positive attitude.		
I have prepared a takeaway to leave my audience.		

You should have answered yes to each item in the checklist. Work toward correcting any negative answers.

Exercise: Evaluate Your Presentation

Complete the following self-evaluation exercise by referring to a talk or a presentation you recently gave:

1. Do you believe the audience felt the information presented was credible? Why or why not?

_____

_____

_____

_____

_____

_____

2. Do you feel the audience connected with you? If not, why not? _____

_____

_____

_____

_____

3. Did you present the information in a logical manner, or did audience members seem confused?

_____

4. Did you emphasize major points several times throughout the presentation to reinforce your audience's memory of them? If you did not, why not?

_____

_____

_____

_____

5. Did you use visual aids? If so, were they effective? Why or why not?

_____

_____

_____

_____

_____

6. Did you remain focused on your subject throughout the presentation? _____

7. Did you recap your key points at the end of the talk? _____

8. Did you give the audience a takeaway (handout, brochure, sample, and so on)? _____

9. Did the audience members act or react the way you had hoped they would? _____

10. Was your appearance and grooming professional? _____

11. Were you confident? If not, why do you feel you were not? _____

_____

_____

_____

_____

_____

12. Were you aware of using positive gestures? _____

13. Were you aware of using negative gestures? If so, how can you eliminate them in the future?

_____

_____

_____

_____

_____

14. Were you enthusiastic and interesting? If not, how could you create interest the next time?

_____

_____

_____

_____

15. Did your audience evaluate you? If so, can you incorporate their suggestions in future presentations?

_____

16. How can you improve your presentations in the future?

_____

_____

_____

_____

_____

_____

WRAP UP

At the end of your talk, reiterate your key points and the reasons they are important for your audience. Remind participants what they have gained from your presentation and how it will help them in the future to solve their problems (or make money or perform better, and so on). Give the audience a take-away handout, brochure, sample, or verbal encouragement.

Let the audience know you welcome their comments and suggestions regarding your presentation. Leave them with a way to contact you. Distribute business cards or give them your email address. Chapter 10, "Improving Through Evaluations," provides information on creating evaluations for the audience to complete.

After your next presentation, complete the checklist that follows.

Wrap-Up of Presentation Checklist	Yes	No
I was enthusiastic and energetic.		
I reiterated my key points at the end of my talk.		
I reminded my audience what they gained from the presentation.		
I gave my audience a takeaway (handout, brochure, sample, and so on).		
I let my audience know I welcome comments and suggestions regarding the presentation.		
I provided my audience with a way to contact me.		

You should have answered yes to each item in the checklist. Work toward correcting any negative answers.

Exercise: Create a Takeaway for the Audience

For your next presentation, create a takeaway you can give your audience at the end of your speech. This can be a handout, copies of your slides, a brochure, a business card, a sample, or even a verbal comment.

Exercise: Videotape Your Presentation

Videotape your next presentation if possible. If it is not possible to videotape yourself, ask a trusted friend to attend the presentation and give you an honest critique of your speech and mannerisms. Work on ways to improve weak areas.

CHAPTER 10

Improving Through Evaluations

Evaluations by your audience members are important tools for measuring the effectiveness of your presentation and of you as a speaker. You can have attendees evaluate your presentation for clarity, effectiveness, interest, value, and the like.

Some speakers dread evaluations, but by having audience members evaluate your presentation, you can learn what you are doing right, where you are going wrong, and possibly how you can improve future presentations. Of course, you are looking for honest, constructive evaluations, but remember that evaluation answers are subjective on the part of the people completing them. Do not be discouraged by negative answers. Treat them as learning experiences. If the majority of your evaluations are positive, you know you are on the right track. When the majority of your evaluations are negative, you obviously want to find ways to improve yourself and your materials. Either way, the evaluations provide benefit to you.

AUDIENCE EVALUATIONS

The right assessment of your presentation can let you know to what degree you benefited your audience. Encourage attendees to evaluate your presentation by making it a simple, quick process for them.

You can create an evaluation rating checklist and include it in your handouts or other presentation materials, or you can develop an online survey the audience can complete at their leisure. Encourage people to fill out the evaluation immediately to discourage their possibly forgetting to do so.

Whatever method you choose to gather answers, make it easy for the audience to fill out the evaluation. Limit the number of questions, and use a quick check-off system. Consider the following types of questions, which can be answered on a typical rating scale. For instance, the answers could be rated on a scale of 1 to 5, with 1 being "strongly disagree" and 5 being "strongly agree." Choose 5 to 10 questions that will provide you with beneficial information.

Sample questions include these:

- Did the presentation meet your expectations?
- Was the purpose of the speech clearly conveyed?
- Was the information presented helpful to you?
- Can you immediately use the information presented?
- Was the information presented in a logical way?
- Was the presentation interactive?
- Was the information well researched?
- Was the information up to date?
- Was the supporting information relevant?
- Were the audio-visual aids relevant?
- Was the speaker enthusiastic and interesting?
- Was the speaker knowledgeable in the subject area?
- Did the presenter speak clearly?
- Did the speaker use appropriate gestures and expressions?
- Did the speaker respond appropriately to participants' questions?
- Did the speaker impart new information to you?
- Did the speaker seem to know the audience and their needs?
- Did the speaker present a neat, well-dressed appearance?
- Did the speaker use correct grammar, pronunciation, and language?
- Did the speaker spend enough time on important areas of the topic?
- Did the speaker hold your attention throughout the presentation?
- Did the speaker recap the key points at the end of the presentation?
- Did the speaker welcome your comments and questions?
- Did the speaker answer questions accurately and thoroughly?

✦ Was the meeting room comfortable?

✦ Would you recommend this presentation to others?

✦ Would you recommend this speaker to others?

If you hope to get more detailed information from your participants, you could create an evaluation where they would fill in their answers in more detail. Ask questions such as these:

✦ What was the most useful idea you received from this presentation?

✦ What could the speaker have done to better help you with regard to this topic?

✦ How can this presentation be improved?

✦ Do you have suggestions for improvement for the speaker?

✦ What did you like best about the presentation?

✦ What did you like least about the presentation?

✦ Do you feel the speaker presented the information well? Explain your answer.

✦ Was the presentation valuable to you? Explain your answer.

✦ What are your suggestions for future presentation topics?

✦ How can you best use the information you were given in the presentation?

✦ What will you tell others about this presentation?

Choose the best method for gathering information, dependent on the type of presentation you give, the audience members and their participation, and what you hope to learn.

Exercise: Analyze an Evaluation Form

The next time you attend a presentation, take special note of the evaluation you are given to complete. Do you feel the evaluation directions are clear and the form is easy to fill out? If you will not be attending a presentation in the near future, research online to find a sample speaker evaluation. Critique the evaluation.

SELF-EVALUATIONS

In addition to audience evaluations, you might want to do a self-evaluation following your presentation. Recall your performance, materials, and content. Think about what you feel went well and where you could have done something differently to be more effective. Be honest with yourself.

Ask yourself these questions or similar ones:

✦ How do you think you did?

✦ Do you feel you achieved your objective?

✦ Did you stick to your topic?

✦ Did you reiterate your important points?

- Did you use your visual aids effectively?
- Were you competent operating the equipment?
- Did you notice any mistakes you made?
- Did you know your material well enough?
- Were you relaxed and confident?
- Did the audience react favorably to you?
- Did you welcome comments and questions?
- Did you answer questions accurately and thoroughly?
- Did you recap your key points at the end of the presentation?
- Did you give the audience a takeaway?

Record your answers for future reference. Make a list of the areas where you would like to see improvement, and seek ways to make the improvements.

PEER EVALUATIONS

One way to obtain a reliable, constructive evaluation is to ask a trusted friend or peer to evaluate you following your next presentation. You can use a simple check-off rating sheet or ask more detailed questions, depending on how much information you want to gather.

You could pose questions such as those presented earlier but ask them from the friend's perspective as adapted here:

- How do you think I did overall?
- Do you feel I achieved the objectives I stated at the beginning of the presentation?
- Did I stick to my topic?
- Did I reiterate my important points?
- Did I use my visual aids effectively?
- Did I seem competent operating the equipment?
- Did you notice any mistakes I made?
- Did I appear to know my material well enough?
- Did I seem relaxed and confident?
- Did you feel the audience reacted favorably to me?
- Did I welcome comments and questions?
- Did I answer questions accurately and thoroughly?
- Did I recap my key points at the end of the presentation?
- Would you recommend me to others?

In addition to the preceding questions, you may want to ask your friend to evaluate your mannerisms, gestures, and overall appearance.

Exercise: Have a Friend Evaluate Your Presentation

Using the following checklist with examples of what to gather information about, create an evaluation for your friend to complete after a practice or actual presentation. Include these or other items you feel you will gain the most benefit from learning about.

Evaluation Checklist	Inadequate	Fair	Good	Excellent
Eye contact				
Voice				
Gestures				
Posture				
Relaxed, calm demeanor				
Grooming				
Dress				
Effectiveness				
Credibility				
Knowledge of subject				
Presentation of subject matter				
Use of visual aids				
Speaker held my interest				
Information benefited me				
Would recommend speaker				

General Comments

_____

_____

_____

_____

_____

_____

_____

_____

CREATION OF EVALUATION

All evaluations should have clear, brief directions as well as a place for the name of the person (or session) being evaluated. Include questions specific to your presentation with an appropriate rating scale. Avoid yes or no answers. A mix of questions about the content and the speaker's delivery will provide the widest range of audience reviews.

Arrange the evaluation in an attractive, easy-to-complete format. Include a comment section to encourage participants to leave specific information you might find useful for future presentations. Provide a line for an optional signature.

Complete the following checklist for your next presentation.

Evaluations Checklist	Yes	No
I have prepared an evaluation checklist.		
I have included explicit, specific directions.		
I have included questions about the presenter.		
I have included questions about the content.		
I have included a question about the overall effectiveness of the presentation.		
I have prepared questions about the venue.		
I have included a comment section.		
I have provided a section for an optional signature.		
I have made the evaluation brief and easy to fill out.		
I have encouraged my audience to complete the evaluation of my presentation.		

You should have answered yes to each item in the checklist. Work toward correcting any negative answers.

Exercise: Create an Evaluation

Create a suitable evaluation you can distribute to attendees of your next presentation. Be sure directions are clear, the form is brief and easy to fill out, and the questions are such that the potential answers will benefit you.

ONLINE SURVEYS

There are a number of online surveys that presenters can adapt for their use. These surveys are created and completed electronically. After you create the survey according to your needs, your audience members can then go online to take the survey. This is a quick, efficient way to have participants evaluate you and your presentation.

Remember, the easier you can make it for participants to evaluate the presentation, the more likely they will do it.

Exercise: Research Online Surveys

Check various online surveys for appropriate ones that allow an audience member to evaluate speakers and their presentations. Make a list of the pros and cons with regard to using such a survey for your next presentation.

Exercise: Create an Online Survey

Create an online evaluation for your next presentation that your audience can complete. Include questions regarding content and your delivery of it.

CHAPTER 11

Building a Platform

If you want to increase your speaking engagements, you need to generate an interest in you and your topic. Begin by creating name recognition in your area of expertise. Next, consider building a platform. A speaker's platform is made up of various components intended to provide visibility for you and to establish your distinction as a presenter.

USE PLATFORM COMPONENTS

Any way that you can promote yourself and gain name recognition can be viewed as your platform. Some of the common platforms include websites, social media sites, blogs, radio and television interviews, book/article/newspaper authoring, webinars, speaking engagements, and the like.

Website

Create, or have someone else create, a website to promote your talks and subject area. You can choose a basic or an elaborate site as long as it provides information about you and your area of expertise. Research the websites of other speakers or professionals who have similar interests to get an idea of what to include on your website.

You need not spend a lot of money on a website, but to be effective you want to let people know how you can benefit them if they attend your presentations.

Post a photograph so people have a face to put with your name. Have a professional headshot taken in order to put your best image online. You want to create the appearance of a qualified expert.

Craft an interesting, informative bio. Include your most prominent speaking engagements and other relevant, attention-grabbing details. Add background facts that attest to your being an expert.

Provide contact information, and make it easy for visitors to the site to contact you. For maximum effectiveness, add a feature to your website that allows you to collect email addresses from visitors to your site who are willing to provide them. You can also add a counter to the site to determine how many visitors you have.

Social Media Sites

An online presence is important in today's society where so many people are connected online. Create a profile on the sites you feel will benefit you the most, such as LinkedIn, Facebook, and Twitter to name a few. Research online social media sites to find ones that will benefit you. These sites can provide contacts, possible customers or prospects, and information and discussions on your topic.

Research online social media sites to find people to connect with who share your passion about your topic. Offer to share your expertise with these individuals. Join groups whose members have a similar interest to yours and those that have something to do with your topic. Participate in group discussions.

Use the same photograph on all your online sites so people begin to recognize you. Craft an interesting, informative bio, and provide contact information.

Exercise: Create a List of Social Media Sites

Make a list of social media sites you could join. Select at least one social media site and create an account to join the site.

Blog

Creating a blog and writing about your subject is an ideal way to share your expertise with a number of people and increase awareness of your availability as a speaker. Limiting your blogs to your topic of expertise and avoiding irrelevant personal information will project a professional image. Update the blog on a regular basis to keep people coming back.

Use the same photograph for your blog as you do on your online sites. Craft an interesting, informative bio, and provide contact information.

Some easy-to-use blog sites allow you to create a blog without much skill; many of them are free. Researching how to build a blog and reading other people's blogs will help you become accustomed to how they work.

Exercise: Analyze Speaker Websites and Blogs

Analyze the websites and blogs of other speakers to determine if you can create a similar website or blog. If possible, create a website. If you already have a website, analyze how your site measures up to those of other speakers.

Exercise: Create a Blog

If you do not have a blog, start one; write and post information about your topic.

Radio and Television Interviews

Aim for wide appeal and interesting content when called on to give an interview. Is it possible to tie your interview in with a newsworthy issue? Has there been recent interest or an upsurge of interest in your topic? Is the topic one that is always newsworthy?

If your topic is not presently in the news, can you find something about your presentation to tie to a current issue? For instance, can you encourage your audience to recycle their handouts, water bottles, and so on in order to think "green"?

Articles, Newsletters, and Books

After you become an expert on your topic, write journal, newsletter, magazine, and newspaper articles and submit them. You might also compose white papers and author books on your subject.

Start your own newsletter and fill it with information about your topic as well as other subjects that might interest your readers.

Exercise: Create a List of Article Topics

Make a list of possible ways to slant articles on your topic(s) for possible inclusion in a variety of publications.

Exercise: Create a Media List

Make a list of possible journals, newsletters, magazines, and newspapers for which you could write articles.

Webinars

Today many speakers offer webinars to air their presentations online. These webinars are offered to participants for free or at a cost. Do an online search if you want to learn more about recording and offering webinars. Check out the webinars other speakers offer.

Tips for Building a Platform

- Create a website.
- Join social media sites.
- Write articles.
- Write a printed book or ebook.
- Hold a contest during your presentation or on your website and give away something of value.
- Create a newsletter and ask your audience and online followers to sign up for it to keep up on the latest news regarding you and your subject.
- Create an email list from your presentation attendees and online followers; email them a list of tips once a month or so.
- Organize workshops and events of your own.
- Create business cards and brochures.

Complete the following checklist.

Building a Platform Checklist	Yes	No
I am an expert in my subject area.		
I have considered the best ways to build my platform.		
I have created or am considering creating a website.		
I have joined social media sites.		
I have written or am considering writing articles.		
I have written or am considering writing a newsletter.		

You should have answered yes to each item in the checklist. Work toward correcting any negative answers.

Exercise: Create a Platform Building Plan

Develop a plan for building a platform. Consider topics on which you are an expert and the types of audiences to which you would like to present.

Exercise: Design a Platform

Determine how you would like to build a platform in the future by completing the following exercise.

1. What is your area of expertise? _____

2. To whom would you like to offer your expertise (for example, companies, schools, individuals, or local community organizations)? _____

   _____

   _____

   _____

3. If you have a website, what content do you have? What visuals? If you do not have a website but plan to have one in the future, what content and visuals will you include?

   _____

   _____

   _____

   _____

   _____

   _____

   _____

4. If you already have a blog, what kind of articles do you post? If you do not have a blog now but will in the future, what kind of articles will you post? _____

   _____

   _____

   _____

   _____

   _____

5. What social media sites have you joined or would you be interested in joining?

   _____

   _____

   _____

Speaking Engagements

To garner speaking engagements, you should prepare proposals for each topic on which you are an expert. Your proposal should include a brief summary of the topic and the length of the presentation. Include a bio that clearly details your expertise. Ask yourself, "What makes you the right person to deliver this presentation?"

Exercise: Develop a Proposal

Develop a proposal for each of the topics about which you would like to speak.

BRAND YOURSELF

Think about how you can brand yourself. Branding is a way of getting people to remember you. One way to do that is to consistently project the same image. Use the same name and picture on all your materials and online sites so people become familiar with them. If you have a logo, use it consistently.

You can also create name recognition with a particular subject(s) if you prefer. For instance, direct all your efforts into being the number-one expert on a particular topic, and then let people know it any way you can.

Complete the following checklist.

Branding Checklist	Yes	No
I have decided how to brand myself to increase my visibility.		
I have decided on the methods I will use to brand myself.		
I have used the same name and photograph for my online and offline presence.		

You should have answered yes to each item in the checklist. Work toward correcting any negative answers.

Exercise: Develop a Plan for Branding Yourself

Develop a plan for branding yourself. Consider your areas of expertise and how you would like to be remembered for your speeches and presentations.